Honest to God

Christian Zionists Confront 10 Questions
Jews Need Answered

By

Pastor Victor L. Styrsky

Forward by
David Brog
author "Standing With Israel"

ARTZY
BOOKS
NEW YORK ◆ JERUSALEM ◆ LONDON

Go to www.cufi.org
to join us in our efforts
to strengthen United States support of Israel.

You may contact Pastor Victor at:
vstyrsky@yahoo.com

Honest to God
Christian Zionists Confront 10 Questions Jews Need Answered

Published by ARTZY BOOKS

Text Copyright © 2009 Pastor Victor L. Styrsky
Cover and Book Design: Benjie Herskowitz
Editors: Judy Lash Balint and Sara Rosenbaum
Editorial and Production Director: Daniella Barak

Soft Cover ISBN: 978-1-934440-49-0

Email: sales@devorapublishing.com
Web Site: www.devorapublishing.com

Printed in the United States of America

~ This book is dedicated to my magnificent father,
Alfred B. Styrsky ~

He rests peacefully and I miss him.

Contents

Foreword		vii
Preface		xi
Introduction:	Twenty-five Years of Supporting Israel	1
Prologue:	Intimate Collisions	13
Question 1:	"Does the Christian community have the patience for us?"	21
Question 2:	"Do Christians still hate us because we don't believe in Jesus?"	53
Question 3:	"What is your *real* agenda in reaching out to the Jews?"	67
Question 4:	"What can we do about Christians 'targeting' us and our children?"	83
Question 5:	"Why don't you educate the anti-Israel churches?"	97
Question 6:	"How are you Christian Zionists trying to affect Israeli politics?"	123
Question 7:	"Do you really believe all the Jews are going to hell?"	155
Question 8.	"You love your enemies? How can you love the terrorists that are killing our children in Israel?"	173
Question 9:	"What would you say if a Jew told you he wanted to convert to Christianity?"	205
Question 10:	"What is your deepest prayer for the Jewish people?"	219
Epilogue:	One Last Story	223

Foreword

In the early years of this decade, I worked for Senator Arlen Specter as his Chief Counsel and, later, his Chief of Staff. Senator Specter represents Pennsylvania, a state with a significant Jewish community largely concentrated in the urban areas of Philadelphia and Pittsburgh. It is also a state with a large and vibrant evangelical Christian community spread throughout the smaller cities and rural communities of the state's middle section.

Over the years, I noticed an extremely interesting phenomenon. Whenever there would be a terrorist attack in Israel, or an anti-Semitic incident in Europe, my phone would light up with calls from constituents back in Pennsylvania. But, to my surprise, a majority of these calls came not from our Jewish constituents in the cities, but from our Christian constituents in the middle of the state. These evangelical Christians were upset that Jewish blood was being spilled, and they wanted Senator Specter to do something about it. There was no mistaking the sincerity and depth of their concern.

As a Jew raised in the northeast, however, I had what I have come to learn is a typical reaction to this outpouring of Christian concern: I was immediately suspicious. Throughout our long and often tragic history, we Jews have not always been well loved by our gentile neighbors. As a result, we have developed a deep-seated skepticism bordering on paranoia when it comes to their intentions. Unable to believe that Christians would support us out of love or solidarity, we search for their "ulterior motive." And if no such ulterior motive exists, we invent one. In Jewish and secular circles, an absurd conventional wisdom maintains that evangelicals support Israel only to convert Jews now or to speed an Armageddon which will bring our ultimate conversion or destruction.

Yet something about these cynical explanations for Christian support simply didn't ring true to me. These dark motives did not match the sincerity and love that I had seen in the eyes and heard in the voices of so many Christian friends. It seemed to me that there had to be more to the story.

Thus I began the research that formed the basis of my book, *Standing with Israel*. As I learned more about the topic, it became increasingly clear to me that the conventional wisdom about Christian support for Israel was an urban myth, without any connection to the truth. Having been the victims of so many slanders about our own faith, we Jews must do better than to passively accept such slanders when they are made against others. Far from wanting to speed our demise, evangelical Christians who stand with Israel today are nothing less than the theological heirs of the religious righteous gentiles who risked their lives to save Jews from the Holocaust.

C8C3⅀℘

After writing my book, I was intellectually convinced that evangelical Christians are real and sincere friends without ulterior motive. But, I must confess, my heart had not kept up with my head. After having grown up with so much suspicion, I did not quickly let my guard down. It was with tense shoulders and crossed arms that I spoke to actual Christian Zionists.

Then I met Pastor Victor Styrsky. We appeared together on a panel at a pro-Israel conference. Here, in front of me, was a flesh-and-blood example of the latter-day righteous gentile I had written about in my book. Here was a man who was visibly pained by the history of Christian anti-Semitism that he knew so well. Here was a man who wanted not only to mourn the tragedies of the past, but to change the future. Here was a man who felt a dedication to the Jewish people and Israel every bit as emotional, deep and real as my own.

It did not take long until we had recruited Victor into the leadership of Christians United for Israel. But even more importantly, it did not take long until Victor had become one of my dearest friends and closest brothers. It is hard to maintain psychological distance when someone shares your heart. Victor was one of my first personal connections in the Christian world, and through Victor I have come to make so many more.

I therefore am thrilled that Victor has finally put pen to paper and shared his warm and oversized heart with a broader audience. It is one thing for me, a Jew, to describe what motivates Christian support for

Israel. It is quite another thing for a Christian supporter of Israel to share his beliefs and thoughts directly. This book is a valuable contribution to what is still a far too limited literature.

I strongly encourage my fellow Jews to take the time to read this book. Throughout all of the lonely centuries, we have prayed for more understanding, appreciation and love from our gentile neighbors. Today, in America, this prayer has been answered in so many ways, including the rise of millions of pro-Israel Christians. Before we dismiss this outpouring of support on the basis of myths and misinformation, we must at least give our friends a hearing, and make an effort to understand them. Victor Styrsky has saved you the trouble of trying to piece together the thinking of Christian Zionists – it is all in his book. Start reading; you might just like what you see.

This book is also a valuable resource for Christians. Supporting Israel, and working with the Jewish community, is a most challenging enterprise. Religion, politics, and a troubled history will place many stumbling blocks in your path. Victor's experience from twenty-five years of pro-Israel work will help clear the way for you. It is a most effective primer.

I must warn you. Victor is harder on his fellow Christians than I would ever be. I have argued that pro-Israel Christians in America today have nothing whatsoever to do with the Christians who persecuted Jews years ago in distant lands. Victor strongly, and consistently, disagrees with me and assumes responsibility for anti-Semitic acts done in the name of his Savior. I understand that Christians are unfamiliar with Jews and our sensitivities and that it will take time before we have bridged these gaps. Victor is often impatient when Christians unwittingly insult Jewish sensibilities. Yet while I may disagree with Victor's position, I am by no means surprised by it. It is just like Victor to demand more of himself, and of his fellow Christians, than others would.

ॐ๏ॐ๏

We in Christians United for Israel stress that what we share as Christians and Jews far outweighs what we have allowed to separate us. We believe that through our work we can bridge an ancient gap and heal a centuries-old wound. We believe that in so doing we bring joy to the God of Abraham, Isaac and Jacob whom we all worship. This journey of Christian and Jewish reconciliation has been one of the most fulfilling and inspiring of my life. I hope you will choose to join us on this journey. I can think of few better ways of beginning than with the book you are about to read.

David Brog, 2009

Preface

We had just finished a four-hour breakfast with some new friends in Yorba Linda, California, when one of them suggested, "Pastor Victor, you need to write a book."

I glibly answered, "And we could have crayons included with it?!"

"I'm serious, brother," he answered.

In the twenty-minute drive to the airport, he and his wife launched into a tag-team assault on my justifiable resistance to their absurd notion. But by the time my wife and I exited their car, the outline for a book was scribbled on my heart.

My closest friends soon added their encouragement to the project and supplied research materials, prayers and helpful criticism throughout the creative process. I asked the people God has so kindly surrounded me with to watch for signs of self-righteousness or unrighteous anger in my thoughts. I begged them for their candid responses and they brought them to me – and the fact that I don't like any of them anymore has nothing to do with their opinion of my writing (just kidding).

They found a sense of impatience and sadness throughout many of the chapters.

I am impatient with and jealous for, my Christian faith.

And I am sad as I write; chiefly because of the decades I have spent as a Christian supporter of Israel and my slowness through many of those years to embrace the Christian truths I present within this book.

I thank my mother and father for their unfailing love and the Christian lives that won me over without a word, my wife and dearest friend, Marita, for being my greatest advocate and "the lifter of my head" whenever God needs additional hands to do so, my precious 'preacher's kids' children; Richard, Asher, Simon, and Sterling for being unending sources of joy and for enduring the painfully slow and ongoing transformation of their father; my little sister Lou Anne who helped me deliver newspapers at 6:00 AM over forty years ago and has continued to support me with my every venture since then (including editing my writing); Don Morsey, the first Christian to disciple me and the man who taught me of God's great love for the Jewish people; Ruth Brandt, a most precious friend and the Jewish Matriarch of Jewish/Christian relations in Sacramento, California, whose love for us launched our little Friday night dinner group into the center of Christian Zionism in the United States; George and Lisa who planted the seed of writing this book and watered it with their encouragement, Roger, Kelly, Randy, Linda and Julie who breathed life into my wife and me during a time of testing in our desert journey and who continue to be our best friends; Charles and Rhonda for the library of books, ponderous thoughts, and truckloads of encouragement they deliver to me; Pastor Jay for his love, warnings and wisdom; Cantor Avi for loving Torah and loving me, Rabbi Joseph, Rabbi Mendy, Rabbi Yossi and Rabbi Isaac for loving me and helping me 'learn,' Pastor John and Diana Hagee who reached out to Marita and me and called us 'beloved' when we were cast aside by others, David Brog who has changed our lives and captured a large portion of our hearts, the countless Christian friends who love, support, and understand us and our work; my dear Muslim neighbors who have loved and taught me, and the many rabbis, cantors and treasured Jewish friends from all around the world who we are blessed to jealously love and call part of our family.

Pastor Victor L. Styrsky

Introduction

Twenty-five Years of Supporting Israel

My decision to write this book is born out of the persistent encouragement of my Jewish and Christian friends. The endeavor results from puzzling and painful discoveries I have made as an evangelical Christian Zionist speaking before many Jewish audiences all around the country.

Through the mysterious way of the Almighty, I have had the distinct privilege of being one of the few evangelical Christians to address Jewish leaders and members of AIPAC at numerous summits and conferences throughout the United States. From synagogues and Jewish homes to student leadership at New York University to University of Texas-Austin campuses, I have preached and listened to, laughed and wept with Jewish audiences as we examine the past, present, and future of our two communities.

The people attending these events have consistently posed questions about Christianity's horrific historic abominations. These audiences are equally perplexed by Christian present-day thinking about the Jewish people. Without fail, their feedback includes accounts of the arrogant and ignorant answers commonly received from well-meaning Christians, confirming their worst and most feared suspicions concerning Christians. I have been the recipient of numerous excruciating personal narratives from Jews whose religious interchanges with Christians commonly reveal a pattern of dialogue that left my new acquaintances in disbelief, confusion, and outrage.

1

Astonishing Ignorance Within Christianity

A petite Jewish woman once inquired of me at a parlor meeting on behalf of the American Israel Public Affairs Committee (AIPAC), "Pastor, I know an evangelical Christian who seems to be very nice, and he explained to me that you believe the Jewish children murdered in the Holocaust are now in hell. Is that really what you teach in your churches?"

"He seems to be very nice?" I thought to myself while trying not to curse or cry.

Is so little expected of the Christian community by the Jews that simply conversing with them now qualifies us as being "nice"?

In a dreadfully perverse way, perhaps, this Christian was being "nice" by imparting his vicious and ignorant judgment rather than inflicting physical violence in his self-righteous arrogance..."nice" when compared to the horrors of our past behavior toward the Jews.

Through painful and illuminating stories from more than twenty-five years of interactions with Jewish people who are dismayed and yet hopeful because of Christian supporters' professed "love" for them, I examine each of the "10 questions Jews need answered." After exposing the standard and often alarming replies communicated by many members of the Christian community, I then offer alternative responses that are Biblically sound, compassionate, and comprehensible for our Jewish 'elder brethren of the faith.'

Not only do I hope to bring an accurate understanding of the emerging Christian Zionist faith to my Jewish readers, but I also hope to dislodge the crushing, self-imposed burden of "preaching the Good News" that Christians so often drag around with them like a ton of bricks. Believers in the New Testament are promised that the cross of Christ is an easy yoke and light burden; yet we frequently hurl splinter-filled planks upon those who inquire of our convictions. We have a consistent record of that approach throughout our entire history with the Jewish people.

At a wedding reception recently, I sat next to a nominally pro-Israel Christian. During our conversation, I was astonished to hear that the young man had never heard of Europe's pogroms. *I hear you: How do you start chatting about the pogroms of Europe at a wedding celebration?* In my customary fervor, I began reciting the history of the Crusades, the Inquisition, the darkened and anti-Semitic heart of Martin Luther.

He suddenly interrupted me, "Pastor Victor, where are you getting all this stuff?!"

"What do mean, where am I getting it?" I answered, trying to figure out if he was serious.

"Well," he continued respectfully, "it sounds like an Internet hoax to me."

My wife and I arrived home from the wedding party around midnight, but I immediately went to my Christian friend's house to leave a copy of David Brog's excellent book, *Standing With Israel* (FrontLine, 2006) on his porch.

I wish I could say this type of historic ignorance within the Christian community is uncommon. Astonishingly, it is not.

What Is A Christian Zionist?

Christian Zionist: a member of the Christian faith who believes in the eternal Biblical covenants God made with Abraham, Isaac, and Jacob. Among these promises include the gifting of the land of Israel to the descendents of these Jewish patriarchs.

This book briefly covers my twenty-five years as a Christian Zionist through personal experiences of loving the Jewish people, the land of Israel, and the Jewish carpenter from Nazareth who extraordinarily changed and undoubtedly saved my life.

My religious birth began in my rock-and-roll hippy commune days of the 1970s and continues through 2009 with my experiences as an evangelical Christian Zionist and my encounters as the California Director of CUFI, Christians United For Israel.

An ironic twist included in this story: As a pastor and Christian Zionist, I have lived with my family in the midst of a very devout, Pakistani Sunni Muslim community in Oak Park, California, for over eleven years.

In *Honest To God: Christian Zionists Confront 10 Questions Jews Need Answered*, I confront the near-irreparable havoc that many well-meaning Christians inflict upon the hearts of God's biblically proclaimed "chosen people" through superficial and inaccurate rhetoric about our faith as it relates to them as Jews. These chapters contain accounts of Christian Zionism awakening in the contemporary church, as well as of the church's ongoing apathy and anti-Semitic arrogance toward the Jews and the land of Israel.

The Christian Curse

For over 1,900 years, hordes of those carrying the banner of Christianity have betrayed the Jewish people.

Appallingly betrayed them – over and over and over again.

Betrayed not only by bankrupt souls in clothes of self-righteous aberration who perpetrated the Crusades and the Inquisition, but also betrayed by the Christian societies of Spain and Germany, Poland, and – much of the rest of the world. After feasting on the fruits of Jewish ingenuity and brilliance brought to countless aspects of living, these anti-Semites, by the darkened reasoning of their collective jealous and wicked hearts, disdainfully cast the Jews out of cities built by their own hands, into uninhabitable ghettos or a continued Diaspora.

For my Christian readers:

The dispersion of Jews outside of Israel from the sixth century B.C., when they were exiled to Babylonia, until the present time. From the Greek, *diaspeirein*, "to scatter."

I empathize with the pain, disbelief, and fear generated in the hearts of many Jews because of the unrelenting Christian sins committed against them. I feel their anguish as strongly as I feel the peace and strength garnered from the deepest tenets of my Christian faith. These two paradigms battle within me, often pressing me through the day, hounding me in the night, and awakening beside me in the morning. I have touched the still raw wounds, oozing with suspicion and distrust, of Holocaust survivors, rabbis, Jewish college students, Jewish children and their terrified parents, an infection left by years of wickedness from perverse saints marching under the banner of Christianity.

The silence of the church during the Holocaust absolutely bewilders the Jewish community still today; as does the aggressiveness of the Christian attempts to convert Jews without showing any apparent awareness or understanding of why conversion is such an abominable concept to them.

I have been afforded an intimate view of these gaping, angry holes in the lives of many precious Jewish people through the friendships I have developed over the years. Only because of the candid questions presented within the privileged sanctity of cautious trust have I glimpsed the sociological mayhem Christians have erected between our two communities.

In honesty, I have not always perceived or been moved so deeply over my friends' torment. But I am today. And I remember the journey that has brought me here. I'm determined to gather my Christian brethren to this place, this place of attempting comprehension of the Christian curse that has been cast upon God's firstborn, the children of Abraham, Isaac, and Jacob.

Sins of Our Ancestors...Sins of Our Brothers

A very precious and brilliant Jewish friend repeatedly contends, "Pastor Victor, you evangelical Christians of today have nothing at all in common with those calling themselves Christians during the Crusades, or the Inquisition, or the pogroms of Europe."

I thank him for his kindness, but each time I must and do absolutely disagree.

We are connected to those Christians.

Of course we are.

For, we too carry the name of the carpenter from Nazareth who has affected our lives in such a remarkable way.

We are, by spiritual bloodline, tethered to the rabid insanity spit from the mouth and scratched from the pen of our patriarchal Protestant reformer Martin Luther in his diatribe, *On the Jews and Their Lies*. We contemporary Christians are as linked to the deadly cold silence of the American church during the Holocaust as we are to the current disengagement and anti-Semitic ramblings of liberal Christian churches. Former President Jimmy Carter is, by his confirmed "faith in Christ," an anti-Semitic Christian brother and we are all related through and by the name Christians call the Name above all Names.

Through the eyes of many Jews, and by our Christian salvation-through-faith theology, we are connected with those who carry and call upon the name of Jesus, in the present and in the past. By our confession of faith in Him, we share in the shame of our reprobate brethren and we should feel our own shame for not making the admission.

"But that was the Catholic Church!"

"There were some Christians that helped Jews during WWII!"

"I'm not responsible for what others have done!"

If you are a Christian, and these are your immediate responses, then I implore you to read this book. Until we embrace the realities of how the Church's failures have exiled the Jewish people from the mercies we have been commanded to extend them, we will not be capable of fulfilling God's heart cry to comfort them.

Isaiah 40:1: Comfort ye, comfort ye My people, saith your God.

Having been a pastor and lived in the church for most of the past thirty years, I have sadly found few who believe or grieve over these realities. Even fewer seem to know much, if anything at all, about this atrocious and bloody history of the Church.

My Jewish friends incredulously ask, "Come on, how can someone not know? How can Christians not be aware of the 1,900 years of the atrocities executed against us in the name of their Christian savior?! I just can't believe it."

My answer to them on our behalf is embarrassing, shocking, and true.

Much of the Christian community is more than woefully ignorant of church history. Pastors don't preach it; congregants don't study it. The outcome of this willful and pathetic ignorance adds to the rising evidence of our inability to mature as a faith community. To make matters worse, many Christians believe, by uninformed or misinformed default, that the history of the Jews ended at the death and resurrection of Christ and that, because of their infidelities as God's chosen people, we Christians have replaced them.

"Really?" I ask.

"God grew tired of the Jews' failures, removed His Name from them and placed it exclusively upon us?" I sarcastically intone to my Christian brethren.

"And you think you can make a case that Christians have done better than Jews in obeying the Almighty?" I mock.

Let's consider: "Did God really tire of the Jews and their failures and reneg on all the promises He made them?"

We are warned by the Apostle Paul, as he writes to Christians concerning the mystery within God's eternal love for the Jews:

Romans 11:1, 25:

> "*I say then, God has not rejected His people, has He? May it never be! ... I do not want you to be ignorant of this mystery, brothers; so that you may not be conceited, Israel has experienced a hardening in part until the full number of the Gentiles has come in. And so all Israel will be saved...*"

Is there any form of conceit more insidious than the unabated persecution of a people solely based upon them not sharing your religious beliefs?

Uncommon Christian Behavior

The Jewish community is well aware of, and forever grateful to, the righteous gentiles who throughout our sordid Christian history gave their lives to protect Jewish lives. The Jews have built numerous monuments on behalf of these heroes of the faith.

History has accurately and permanently recorded the actions of these saints as exhibiting extraordinary – and uncommon Christian behavior.

Conceit in the Church Continues

I lost much of my youthful innocence in the world of rock and roll. Then, as a pastor for twenty-five years, I was stripped of what naiveté remained by the shock of discovering the sins within the church; the sins recorded throughout our history, the enormity of the sins congregants reveal to their leaders in confidence, and the secret lives of hypocritical pastors.

My wife and I writhe in dismay every time one of our national Christian leaders is caught and reported on the news as living a life of righteous pretense. We scream at the television, "YOU'RE KILLIN' US OUT HERE!!" These Christian men, who are exposed for committing the very same sins in the night that they have howled against on Sunday mornings, are by lineage my brothers in Christ.

I scream at them, I share their shame and dismay, I forgive them and I cry for them and their families. I do realize that "there but for the grace of God," and so on. But what a fearful negligence of the church for not stepping up to the local news microphones and declaring to the public, "We are sick, ashamed, and angry over this news. We ask for God's and your forgiveness. We do love Pastor _____ and ask that you pray for his family, for him, and for our church community."

Humility is *not* one of the qualities for which the Christian community is known. Yet, along with love, humility is supposed to be one of the very basic elements of our faith.

One night we were watching the Larry King Show as one of our most highly esteemed Christian leaders was being interviewed. He was asked regarding a fallen prominent pastor whose homosexual lifestyle the man had been hiding from his wife and family.

"Do you think this was hypocritical of Pastor_____?" King scowled.

"No I don't," was the gentle reply. "He had been fighting against these dark impulses for a long – blah, blah, blah," the Christian guest submitted.

We hollered at the television, "Are you kidding me?? The devil made him do it??"

"YOU'RE KILLIN' US OUT HERE!!"

The only honest answer for the matter is, "Yes. Of course he was being hypocritical. Pastor _____'s actions are the epitome of hypocrisy."

Is our Christian faith so frail that admitting our failures is paramount to the surrender of our convictions? Those observing us may conclude so.

In regard to the church's relationship with the Jewish people, this lack of integrity is much more insidious than our grandiose self-righteousness. Centuries of massacring Jews exemplify the supreme incarnation of arrogance.

For the Christian reading this who is now protesting –

"But we've been forgiven! We have the promises Jesus made to us! WE have His precious promises! We have the New Covenant!"

I answer: The Jews also have precious promises.

God's Promises to the Jews

The Jewish people have promises made to them unilaterally by the God of Abraham, Isaac, and Jacob, the God our Jesus called "Abba."

For my Christian readers:

The Aramaic word for "Father," "my Father," together with the Greek equivalent, occurs three times in the New Testament. It is an invocation to God, reflecting a close, tender, and personal relationship between the speaker and God. There is nothing specially Christian about this. It was the formula for addressing God that was most familiar to the religious Jews of the New Testament times.

Jesus's Father swore on His own name that He would keep these promises with the Jewish people. He promised He would keep the promises forever. Many of these promises were based, not on the faithfulness or works of the Jewish people (just like many of His promises to us), but were solely based upon His Name, His love for the Jewish people, and His resolve to demonstrate that He is God. He has made and will keep these promises in order to show all the nations of the world that He is God alone, that He is good, and that He alone is able to make the Jews a holy people, for they are unable to attain holiness on their own merit. (Just like us.)

Ezekiel Chapter 36:22-28:

> *Therefore say unto the house of Israel: Thus saith the Lord God: I do not this for your sake, O house of Israel, but*

for My holy name, which ye have profaned among the nations, whither ye came.

And I will sanctify My great name, which hath been profaned among the nations, which ye have profaned in the midst of them; and the nations shall know that I am HaShem, saith the Lord God, when I shall be sanctified in you before their eyes.

For I will take you from among the nations, and gather you out of all the countries, and will bring you into your own land.

And I will sprinkle clean water upon you, and ye shall be clean; from all your uncleannesses, and from all your idols, will I cleanse you.

A new heart also will I give you, and a new spirit will I put within you; and I will take away the stony heart out of your flesh, and I will give you a heart of flesh.

And I will put My spirit within you, and cause you to walk in My statutes, and ye shall keep Mine ordinances, and do them.

And ye shall dwell in the land that I gave to your fathers; and ye shall be My people, and I will be your God. And I will save you from all your uncleannesses...

"And that 'New Covenant' you're citing?" I continue.

"That New Covenant we're all so proud about when we're supposed to be humble and broken over it?" I remind my Christian brethren.

"That covenant was first declared by God through the Jewish prophet Jeremiah, and that covenant is a promise made to the Jews," I finish.

Jeremiah 31:31-37:

Behold, the days come, saith HaShem, that I will make a new covenant with the house of Israel, and with the house of Judah; not according to the covenant that I made with their fathers in the day that I took them by the hand to bring them out of the land of Egypt; forasmuch as they broke My covenant, although I was a lord over them, saith HaShem.

But this is the covenant that I will make with the house of Israel after those days, saith HaShem, I will put My law in their inward parts, and in their heart will I write it; and I will be their God, and they shall be My people; and they shall teach no more every man his neighbor, and every man his brother, saying: 'Know HaShem'; for they shall all know Me, from the least of them unto the greatest of them, saith HaShem; for I will forgive their iniquity, and their sin will I remember no more.

Thus saith HaShem, Who giveth the sun for a light by day, and the ordinances of the moon and of the stars for a light by night, who stirreth up the sea, that the waves thereof roar, HaShem of hosts is His name: If these ordinances depart from before Me, saith HaShem, then the seed of Israel also shall cease from being a nation before Me for ever.

Thus saith HaShem: If heaven above can be measured, and the foundations of the earth searched out beneath, then will I also cast off all the seed of Israel for all that they have done, saith HaShem.

For my Christian readers:

HaShem is a Hebrew word for *God*, meaning "The Name." Jews use it as a substitute word when referring to God in situations other than prayer or worship. This is done to honor the Almighty and prevent using the Name of God in vain.

Jewish History Did Not End At The Cross

Our Christian history cannot be changed, but I believe we can be. We will not be changed by some novel spiritual truth that can be packaged and then presented from the pulpits of America, but rather transformed by beginning to accept as absolute truth the promises God has established in the scriptures – all the promises in the Bible, not just the ones made to the Christian church.

A current inaccuracy in segments of Christianity stems from the thinking that Jewish history ended at the cross of Christ. These believers are taught that the New Testament began at this conclusion of Jewish history, thus completing and annulling all the Old Testament's application.

As an evangelical Christian, i.e., a proponent of the Bible being wholly literal and inspired by God, I believe that the God of Abraham, Isaac, and Jacob made numerous covenants with the Jewish people that He swore to be eternal.

I can hear some of my Christian friends protesting again, "JESUS – what about JESUS?"

What about Him? I am a Christian Zionist, but I am not less of a Christian because I have become more of a Zionist. I am persuaded that everyone, Jew and gentile, needs the promised Messiah. I believe that Jesus is the Son of David and savior of the whole world. But my Jewish readers already know what I believe about Jesus because of my identification as a Christian.

The problems in our relations with the Jewish people stem from the tribulations we caused them, and have absolutely nothing to do with the son of Mary and stepson of Joseph. The contentious wall of separation between our communities is our fault, the result of our ancient and current Christian record of exceedingly arrogant, hypocritical, and wicked anti-Semitic actions toward the sons and daughters of Abraham, Isaac, and Jacob, "the apple of God's eye."

I pray this book illuminates for my Christian readers a graceful way to give honest answers concerning the tenets of our faith. For my Jewish readers, I pray this book will be a source of exceeding hope for a future with trustworthy Zionist Christian friends.

The style and content of *Honest To God: Christian Zionists Confront 10 Questions Jews Need Answered* is not an intensely theological or exhaustive historic study guide, but rather a Christian primer for touching the apple of God's eye – without poking it out.

Prologue

Intimate Collisions

My friend spent more than three decades as a teaching professor and president at one of America's highly regarded Christian seminaries. His name is listed as a noted scholar and contributor within the pages of numerous best-selling study Bibles. The professor knows exactly what he believes within the theology of the Hebrew and Greek Scriptures and has taught countless others these truths for well over fifty years.

He knew what he believed until the day his daughter tested his theology.

She had married young, and the marriage never took hold. Years of tears and counseling and immaturity had left this father's daughter a hollow shell of the effervescent woman he had kissed goodbye on her wedding day.

Her husband never hit her nor was he guilty of sexual infidelity. Rather, he was entirely unfaithful in following the commandments to nourish and cherish his wife.

She had spiritually and emotionally died under his watch, and she could not find a way to continue with the non-relationship for another day.

Her father now warned her concerning the gravity of the steps she was considering.

DIVORCE!

This is exactly how his denomination looked upon the act. Divorce was a heavy, dark, disturbing sin and those who succumbed to it were also bound to it for the rest of their natural days. Because his daughter's unfaithful husband had been faithful to his sexual vows, Dad-the-seminary-professor had to warn her that, should she end her marriage in divorce, "she would never be able to marry again."

Isn't that a bit harsh, you ask?

Many evangelicals will answer cavalierly, "Talk to God. It's His Word, not mine!"

Some Christians believe with all their hearts (as did my friend) that this is the definitive word and heart of our Creator concerning divorce and remarriage.

After many more tears and prayers, this young woman embarked upon the only path that left her any hope, divorcing the husband of her youth.

A number of years passed and the wounds of bewilderment, guilt, and shame healed. This revitalized woman once again reflected the zest and joy of life she had known before her malnourished and ill-fated marriage. All was well in her heart and in her home.

And then she fell in love.

It happened at church, and to make things even more difficult, this honorable Christian fellow she fell in love with appeared to be the perfect companion her parents had hoped and prayed for since she was born.

How tragic and too late was the arrival of this godly friend who would have loved, comforted, and cherished until "death do they part."

An additional problem loomed, when her father began loving this man and imagining him as part of the family! A tsunami of conflict swelled within the heart of my theologically sound professor like he had never before experienced.

His convictions concerning divorce and remarriage were being tested for the first time in his life.

Until our theology collides with our life, it remains unproven dogma. It is often comprised of Biblical sound bites and interpretations we have compiled at a safe distance from personal cost for the belief.

Much of the doctrine we adopt without testing is usually augmented by the influence of the religious community around us.

The father wept and prayed as he read the familiar words of Jesus recorded in Matthew, 19:8-9:

> Jesus said to them, "Moses, because of the hardness of your hearts, permitted you to divorce your wives, but from the beginning it was not so. And I say to you, whoever divorces his wife, except for sexual immorality, and marries another, commits adultery; and whoever marries her who is divorced commits adultery."

The professor recounted the many broken-hearted people he had instructed and imprisoned through the rigid adherence to the verse's apparent ironclad decree. It had been to some extent uncomplicated to force upon others what was now utterly unthinkable for his own flesh and blood.

"How could God impose such an irrational life sentence upon my innocent daughter?" he questioned over and over again.

He could no more envision the unbearable prison of inconsistency causing his theological crisis than he could imagine his daughter without this gallant Christian man as her husband.

So he sought a way, and he found it through the testing of his theology. He went back to God and into the Bible he loved, frantically searching for truth like a father seeking after a lost child.

In a nutshell, this was the Christian theological epiphany he experienced:

1) All sin is caused by man's hardness of heart toward God.

2) As Christians, we believe that Jesus atones for and forgives all of our sins, as we ask Him to do so

3) His daughter's divorce was the result of sin. She needed to confess it as such, and she would then be cleansed of it (as with all sin we acknowledge) and be free to marry again.

Merciful God!

The professor just couldn't stop singing the chorus of the old Gospel spiritual:

> *O happy day! O happy day!*
> *When Jesus washed all my sins away!*

How could he have missed the mark for so many years concerning this controversial portion of scripture? How could he have been so callous and blinded in *his* righteousness when dealing with all the others who had tearfully sought his counsel concerning their own marital failings?

How?

It was easy.

Until now, his theology had never collided with the yearnings of his heart. His doctrine regarding divorce had never been tested in the white-hot fire of real love.

End of story: His daughter married and lived very happily ever after. Professor-Grandpa considers his grandchildren and son-in-law amongst the richest blessings God has ever bestowed upon him. My professor friend, now in his mid-70s continues to write and travel the nation, preaching and teaching.

I personally understand the horrifying and long-lasting consequences divorce can inflict upon families and children. My simplification of this one story should not be taken as a suggestion to follow its example to escape the common trials of marriage. For the Christian reader who adheres to the "no remarriage" doctrine of divorce, I suggest you have not yet been tested in this area of your faith. If you associate with a Christian you believe is living in the continued state of adultery by remarrying after a divorce for any cause other than infidelity, then you are sinning by disobeying the following Scripture.

I Corinthians 5:11:

> *But now I am writing you that you must not associate with anyone who calls himself a brother but is sexually immoral...*

Every church has members who have remarried after failed marriages. Some of these marriages include men and women who have gone through a divorce that was not due to infidelity, but rather to other insurmountable problems within the marriage. These "adulterous" Christians take Communion with you, they teach in your Sunday Schools, and they worship with you every Sunday.

The fact that you and your leaders do not root them out and remove them from your midst until they cease from their "immoral" lifestyle makes you as guilty of sin as you believe they are.

What about these marriages that have now produced children? How do you approach and associate with these families and remain true to your interpretation of what Jesus was saying in Matthew 19:8-9? The fact is, you probably don't, but neither do you address the biblical problem this creates within your own theology and life.

My point: It is easy to say we believe something until we are forced to live out our untested theology – when it intimately touches our life.

In the writings of 2 Samuel 12, we find King David about to have his theology tested in a very personal and life-altering way.

In the midst of a normal day, while listening to the concerns of his subjects, King David hears a story so horrendously unjust that it fills him with absolute fury.

> *There were two men in the same city – one rich, the other poor. The rich man had huge flocks of sheep, herds of cattle. The poor man had nothing but one little female lamb, which he had bought and raised. It grew up with him and his children as a member of the family. It ate off his plate and drank from his cup and slept on his bed. It was like a daughter to him. One day a traveler dropped in on the rich man. He was too stingy to take an animal from his own herds or flocks to make a meal for his visitor, so he took the poor man's lamb and prepared a meal to set before his guest.*

There is no need for David to summon his counselors or seek the Almighty in prayer. Unable to contain himself, he shouts out an immediate and righteous judgment in response to the act of savagery that has been committed under his watch.

"As surely as the Lord lives," he vowed, "any man who would do such a thing deserves to die! He must first repay four lambs to the poor man for the one he stole and for having no pity!"

The man commissioned by the Almighty to bring this matter before King David endures his response, and then answers him with...**the rest of the story:**

> Then Nathan the prophet said to David, "You are that man!"
>
> The Lord, the God of Israel, says: "I anointed you king of Israel and saved you from the power of Saul. I gave you your master's house and his wives and the kingdoms of Israel and Judah. And if that had not been enough, I would have given you much, much more. Why, then, have you despised the word of The Lord and done this horrible deed? For you have murdered Uriah the Hittite with the sword of the Ammonites and stolen his wife. From this time on, your family will live by the sword because you have despised me by taking Uriah's wife to be your own."
>
> This is what The Lord says: "Because of what you have done, I will cause your own household to rebel against you. I will give your wives to another man before your very eyes, and he will go to bed with them in public view. You did it secretly, but I will make this happen to you openly in the sight of all Israel..."

"Gulp..." the king silently responds.

David immediately has a change of heart in the matter and humbly replies, "I have sinned against The Lord."

His theology concerning the judgments, righteousness, and mercy of God has just had an intimate collision with his life.

We can see the effects this encounter had on his understanding of the God of Israel by reading Psalm 54 and other songs of praise he wrote in the days that follow this tragic chapter of his life.

I present these stories to my readers because of the great and urgent need for individual, personal reflection by Christians – a self-examination of the authenticity of our love and support for the Jewish people.

I suggest that until our Zionist theology interrupts our lives through intimate collisions with our hearts, it remains untested and adolescent in nature.

Thousands upon thousands of Christian Zionists stand with Israel because it is written in the Bible to do so.

They "love" the Jewish people because they know they should – and this is good.

But you cannot genuinely love what you do not intimately know, nor can you effectively support someone from an emotional distance. Sadly, many Christian Zionists do not have one close Jewish friend.

Absent such relationships, these Christians never eat at Jewish homes, attend Jewish children's birthday parties or bar mitzvahs/bat mitzvahs, or weep in prayer over personal trials afflicting Jewish families. These same Christian supporters of Israel have never received the blessing of a rabbi's prayer for them; nor have they heard, felt, or understood the real fears and hopes of the Jewish people.

Partially due to the Christian emotional distance from personal Jewish friendships, we remain theological, emotionally detached from the Jewish people. These chasms result in causing Jews often to feel like they are nothing more than our conversion targets or our good luck charms. (Genesis 12:3 I will bless those who bless you...)

My journey as a Christian Zionist has awakened me to these ominous relational chasms, as you will see recounted through numerous stories in this book. Please read with patience the apparent detours these personal experiences take, as they are each essential in understanding my responses to these *10 Questions Jews Need Answered*.

I pray this book will touch your life and theology, as well as encourage you to watch for your own paths of intimate encounters as you stand with God's chosen people – the descendants of Abraham, Isaac, and Jacob.

Question 1

"Does the Christian community have the patience for us?"

Standard Christian Answer:
"I have no idea what your question means."

I received a call from The Israel/Christian Nexus and was invited to participate in an event titled "Honest to God: A candid conversation between a rabbi and a pastor."

For my Christian readers:

The *Israel-Christian Nexus* was created in 2002 to bring Christians and Jews together in support of the people and state of Israel. Established by one of Israel's founding fathers and one of its most decorated war heroes, General (ret.) Shimon Erem the mission of the Israel-Christian Nexus is to strengthen the alliance between Jews and Christians in defense of our shared Judeo-Christian values and to educate and mobilize the two communities for sustained action in solidarity with the nation and people of Israel.

The rabbi and I did not rehearse the questions ahead of time, nor

21

did we put any boundaries on the topics that would be discussed. Together we hoped that our interaction would embody exactly what the title had promised.

As the workshop progressed, it grew frighteningly intimate as we tearfully exhausted each other and the allotted time for our presentation.

The rabbi pondered out loud one last question I could tell was of enormous significance to him.

"Pastor?" he cautiously inquired, both dreading and hoping in the answer he might hear.

"Does the Christian community have the patience for us?"

Scanning my cerebral hard disk for any sort of information on how to answer such a troubling concern, I bought myself some time by quipping, "Patience? My wife and I have raised teenagers – you guys are easy!"

Getting Past "Dialogue"

While spending time with a new pastor in town, he and I began talking about the work of Christian Zionists. My heart quickens and my eyes begin to shine whenever I am turned loose on the subject of Christians and Jews. As I spoke of my deep and brotherly love for my Jewish friends, the pastor leaned back in his chair and wrinkling his forehead asked, "So what is the dialogue like when you are speaking with Jews?"

"Dialogue?"

Now that is an incredibly safe, sterile, and strained thought when describing a love relationship.

I don't have "dialogue" with my children. I certainly don't have dialogue within the intimacies of my marriage, and I don't have dialogue when speaking with Jews.

When having fellowship with my Jewish friends, we do so face to face, as equals, as brothers and sisters. And why not? We are the only two faith communities on earth that recognize the God of Abraham, Isaac, and Jacob as our heavenly *Abba*.

For my Christian readers:

The children of my Jewish friends call their fathers *Abba*, as do the children of my Suni Muslim neighbors. Though I have a loving relationship with my Muslim neighbors, I purposly omit them as believers in the God of the Hebrew and New Testament Bible. They are not.

At this point, a number of Christian readers are saying, "Well, I can only have true fellowship with other Christians."

Yea, our history has shown that we think and live that way.

I'm not talking about the "fellowship" of something like interfaith marriages here. Both the Torah and New Testament discourage those unions and I won't perform them.

Neither am I referring to the "fellowship" or communion of our faith. As Christians, we see some faith issues differently than the Torah-loving Jewish community. We, therefore, practice portions of our faith in different ways that may not always be transferable into some aspects of our fellowship with each other.

But I do have fellowship with my Jewish friends over the many truths of God we see as one – many of these truths taught to us by the faithfulness of the Jews!

We have deep fellowship concerning our love, hopes and fears concerning our children and marriages.

I have often had hilarious and pain-filled fellowship with Jewish leaders concerning the tendencies in both our flocks for the sheep to gnaw on their shepherds rather than feast on the Word of God.

Many of my Jewish friends accompany me when I'm ministering in their cities, and my wife and I often attend their synagogue services as well.

Call it what you will, but I experience many times of rich fellowship with my Jewish buddies.

And no matter what you call it, as Christians – until we establish a true bond of love within all of our personal relationships, we are sorely missing the mark set by our Chief Rabbi.

For my Christian readers:

Remembering that Jesus was repeatedly criticized for having "fellowship" with folks outside of his faith community, please re-evaluate the boundaries you have placed around your life when it comes to creating loving relationships with those who are not members of your church association. Sadly, many Christians have very few if any meaningful relationships other than those within the local church they attend.

So..."dialogue"?

Let's leave dialogue for politicians and diplomats.

Honest to God.

"Honest to God... A candid conversation between a rabbi and a pastor," had rocketed way past dialogue as the spirit of God fell upon all of us in the room. Each interaction we shared was drenched with healing tears of hope that appeared to be airborne as our weeping contagiously spread throughout the entire sanctuary. (At one point my wife actually flung a box of tissues on the stage so the rabbi and I could blow our noses and hopefully put an end to our increasingly irritating, unprofessional, and amplified sniffling into the lapel microphones we were wearing.)

Rabbi Isaac faintly smiled and asked again, "Does the Christian community have the patience for us?"

Why would a rabbi, who had been given a free pass on examining the theology and thoughts of a Christian Zionist pastor, ask such an odd question?

As I prayed for understanding I began to comprehend the effects of the innumerable layers of historic decimation of the Jewish people living in Christian societies that begged an answer.

Awareness of this Christian/Jewish record is absolutely essential for an elementary understanding of the rational hesitancy of the Jewish community to fully embrace our new proclaimed love for them.

It may also begin to help each of us in trying to understand the mysterious question my rabbi friend asked in such a gracious manner.

Please – take the time to reflect upon Christianity's horrid, historic testimony and the personal stories of those who were the recipients of our wicked transgressions. As you do, try to grasp the cumulative and heartbreaking wounds this has left upon the Jewish people.

Persecution of Jews by Christians

"The Jews are a nervous people. Nineteen centuries of Christian love have taken a toll." Benjamin Disraeli (1804-1881). England's only Jewish Prime Minister.

170 AD: Notable early Christian apologist, Tertullain taught that the Jews were the "Cains, the murderers, and were rejected as the Chosen People of God." 'Adversus Judaeos.'

220 AD: Origen, one of the most distinguished of the early fathers of the Christian Church, declared the Jews as dangerous enemies of Christians.

306 AD: The church Synod of Elvira banned marriages, sexual intercourse and community contacts between Christians and Jews.

315 AD: Constantine published the Edict of Milan that extended religious tolerance to Christians. Jews lost many rights with this edict. They were no longer permitted to live in Jerusalem, or to proselytize.

325 AD: The Council of Nicea decided to separate the celebration of Easter from the Jewish Passover. They stated: "For it is unbecoming beyond measure that on this holiest of festivals we should follow the customs of the Jews. Henceforth let us have nothing in common with this odious people...We ought not, therefore, to have anything in common with the Jews...our worship follows a...more convenient course...we desire dearest brethren, to separate ourselves from the detestable company of the Jews...How, then, could we follow these Jews, who are almost certainly blinded."

337 AD: Christian Emperor Constantius created a law that made the marriage of a Jewish man to a Christian punishable by death.

339 AD: Converting to Judaism became a criminal offense.

343-381 AD: The Laodicean Synod approved Cannon XXXVIII: "It is not lawful [for Christians] to receive unleavened bread from the Jews, nor to be partakers of their impiety."

367-376 AD: St. Hilary of Poitiers referred to Jews as a perverse people who God has cursed forever. St. Ephroem refers to synagogues as brothels.

379-395 AD: Emperor Theodosius the Great permitted the destruction of synagogues if it served a religious purpose. Christianity became the state religion of the Roman Empire at this time.

380 AD: The bishop of Milan was responsible for the burning of a synagogue; he referred to it as "an act pleasing to God." St. Ambrose calls the synagogue "a place of unbelief, a home of impiety, a refuge of insanity, damned by God Himself."

400 AD: Calling the synagogue a "brothel and theater" and "a cave of pirates and the lair of wild beasts," St. John Chrysostom wrote that "the Jews behave no better than hogs and goats in their lewd grossness and the excesses of their gluttony."

415 AD: The Bishop of Alexandria, St. Cyril, expelled the Jews from that Egyptian city.

415 AD: St. Augustine wrote "The true image of the Hebrew is Judas Iscariot, who sells the Lord for silver. The Jew can never understand the Scriptures and forever will bear the guilt for the death of Jesus."

418 AD: St. Jerome, who created the Vulgate translation of the Bible, wrote of a synagogue: "If you call it a brothel, a den of vice, the Devil's refuge, Satan's fortress, a place to deprave the soul, an abyss of every conceivable disaster or whatever you will, you are still saying less than it deserves."

489-519 AD: Christian mobs destroyed the synagogues in Antioch, Daphne (near Antioch) and Ravenna.

528 AD: Emperor Justinian (527-564) passed the Justinian Code. It prohibited Jews from building synagogues, reading the Bible in Hebrew, assembling in public, celebrating Passover before Easter, and testifying against Christians in court.

535 AD: The Synod of Claremont decreed that Jews could not hold public office or have authority over Christians.

538 AD: The 3rd and 4th Councils of Orleans prohibited Jews from appearing in public during the Easter season. Canon XXX decreed: "From the Thursday before Easter for four days, Jews may not appear in the company of Christians." Marriages between Christians and Jews were prohibited. Christians were prohibited from converting to Judaism.

561 AD: The bishop of Uzes expelled Jews from his diocese in France.

591 AD: Pope St. Gregory the Great decreed that Jews were not to be forced into baptism "lest they return to their former superstition and die the worse for having been born again."

612 AD: Jews were not allowed to own land, to be farmers or enter certain trades.

613 AD: Very serious persecution began in Spain. Jews were given the options of either leaving Spain or converting to Christianity. Jewish children over 6 years of age were taken from their parents and given a Christian education.

692 AD: Canon II of the Quinisext Council stated: "Let no one in the priestly order nor any layman eat the unleavened bread of the Jews, nor have any familiar intercourse with them, nor summon them in illness, nor receive medicines from them, nor bathe with them; but if anyone shall take in hand to do so, if he is a cleric, let him be deposed, but if a layman, let him be cut off."

694 AD: The 17th Church Council of Toledo, Spain defined Jews as the serfs of the prince. This was based, in part, on the beliefs by Chrysostom, Origen, Jerome, and other Church Fathers that God punished the Jews with perpetual slavery because of their responsibility for the execution of Jesus.

722 AD: Leo III outlawed Judaism. Jews were baptized against their will.

830 AD: Agobard, Archbishop of Lyons, wrote anti-Jewish pamphlets in which he refers to Jews as "sons of darkness."

855 AD: Jews were exiled from Italy.

937 AD: Pope Leo VII encouraged his newly appointed archbishop of Mainz to expel all Jews who refused to be baptized.

1010 AD: In Rouen, Orléans, Limoges, Mainz, and Rome, Jews were converted by force, massacred, or expelled.

1050 AD: The Synod of Narbonne prohibited Christians from living in the homes of Jews.

1078 AD: Pope Gregory VII decreed: "Jews could not hold office or be superiors to Christians."

1078 AD: The Synod of Gerona forced Jews to pay church taxes.

1081 AD: Pope Gregory VII wrote to King Alphonso of Spain, telling him that if he allows Jews to be lords over Christians, he is oppressing the Church and exalting "the Synagogue of Satan."

The Crusaders

"In an unheard of and unprecedented outburst of cruelty, they have slaughtered, in this mad hostility, two thousand and five hundred of them; old and young as well as pregnant women. Some were mortally wounded and others trampled like mud under the feet of horses. They burned their books and, for greater shame and disgrace, they exposed the bodies of those thus killed for food to the birds of heaven and their flesh to the beasts of the earth. After hideously and shamefully treating those who remained alive after this massacre, they carried off their goods and consumed them. And in order that they may be able to hide such an inhuman crime under the cover of virtue, and in some way justify their unholy cause, they represent themselves as having done the above and threaten to do worse, on the ground that they (the Jews) refuse to be baptized."

Pope Gregory IX Ugolino, Count of Sefni, c. 1145-1241. From a letter to the Archbishop of Bordeaux and the Bishops of Saintes, Angouleme, and Poitiers, on Sept. 5, 1236. –[Need full citation here] Grayzel, p. 227 ff.

1096 AD: The First Crusade was launched in this year. Although the prime goal of the crusades was to liberate Jerusalem from the Muslims, Jews were a second target. As the soldiers passed through Europe on the way to the Holy Land, large numbers of Jews were challenged: "Christ-killers, embrace the Cross or die!" Twelve thousand Jews in the Rhine Valley alone were killed in the first Crusade. This behavior continued for eight additional crusades until the 9th in 1272. The Jewish chronicler reports: "The enemies stripped them naked and dragged them off, granting quarter to none, save those few who accepted baptism. The number of the slain was eight hundred in these two days." The chronicler Guibert de Nogent reports that the Rouen Crusaders said: "We desire to go and fight God's enemies in the East; but we have before our eyes certain Jews, a race more unfavorable to God than any other."

1099 AD: The Crusaders forced all the Jews of Jerusalem into a central synagogue and set it on fire. Those who tried to escape were forced back into the burning building.

1121 AD: Jews were exiled from Flanders (now part of present-day Belgium).

1130 AD: Some Jews in London allegedly killed a sick man. The Jewish people in the city were required to pay one million marks as compensation.

1146 AD: The Second Crusade began. A French Monk, Rudolf, called for the destruction of the Jews.

1179 AD: Canon 24 of the Third Lateran Council stated: "Jews should be slaves to Christians and at the same time be treated kindly due of humanitarian considerations." Canon 26 stated: "the testimony of Christians against Jews is to be preferred in all causes where they use their own witnesses against Christians."

1180 AD: The French King of France, Philip Augustus, arbitrarily seized all Jewish property and expelled the Jews from the country. There was no legal justification for this action. The Jews were allowed to sell all movable possessions, but their land and houses were stolen by the king.

1189 AD: Jews were persecuted in England. The Crown claimed all Jewish possessions. Most of their houses were burned.

1190 AD: The Third Crusade, led by Richard the Lion-Heart, stirred anti-Jewish fervor and resulted in the mass suicide of the York Jews in Clifford's Tower on March 16.

1205 AD: Pope Innocent III wrote to the archbishops of Sens and Paris that "the Jews, by their own guilt, are consigned to perpetual servitude because they crucified the Lord...As slaves rejected by God, in whose death they wickedly conspire, they shall by the effect of this very action, recognize themselves as the slaves of those whom Christ's death set free..."

1215 AD: The Fourth Lateran Council approved canon laws requiring that "Jews and Muslims shall wear a special dress." They also had to wear a badge in the form of a ring. This was to enable them to be easily distinguished from Christians. This practice later spread to other countries.

1227 AD: The Synod of Narbonne required Jews to wear an oval badge. This requirement was reinstated during the 1930's by Adolf Hitler, who changed the oval badge to a Star of David.

1229 AD: The Spanish Inquisition started. Later, in 1252, Pope Innocent IV authorized the use of torture by the Inquisitors.

1235 AD: Thirty-four Jews were burned to death in Fulda, Germany on a blood-libel charge. (The Jewish blood-libel myth continues to be taught as truth throughout many Muslim countries to this day.)

Blood Libel

In 1144, an unfounded rumor began in eastern England that Jews had kidnapped a Christian child, tied him to a cross, stabbed his head to simulate Jesus' crown of thorns, killed him, drained his body completely of blood, and mixed the blood into matzos (unleavened bread) at the time of Passover. The rumor was started by a Jew, Theobald, who had become a Christian monk. He said that Jewish representatives gathered each year in Narbonne, France and decided in which city a Christian child would be sacrificed.

The boy involved in the 1144 hoax became known as St. William of Norwich. Many people made pilgrimages to his tomb and claimed that miracles had resulted from appeals to St. William. The myth shows a complete lack of understanding of mainline Judaism. Aside from the prohibition of killing innocent persons, the Torah specifically forbids the drinking or eating of any form of blood in any quantity.

However, reality never has had much of an impact on blood libel myths. This rumor lasted for many centuries; even today it has not completely disappeared.

Pope Innocent IV ordered a study in 1247 CE. His investigators found that the myth was a Christian invention used to justify persecution of the Jews. At least four other popes subsequently vindicated the Jews. However, the accusations, trials and executions continued. In 1817, Czar Alexander I of Russia declared that the blood libel was a myth. Even that announcement did not stop the accusations against Jews in that country.

Holy shrines were erected to honor innocent Christian victims, and well into the twentieth century churches throughout Europe displayed knives and other instruments that Jews purportedly used for these rituals.

Caricatures of hunchbacked Jews with horns and fangs were depicted in works of art and carved into stone decorating bridges. Proclaimed by parish priests to be the gospel truth, each recurrence of the blood libel charge added to its credence, thus prompting yet more accusations. This vicious cycle continued to spiral.

Shari Schwartz, Editor's Preface: The Making of a Martyr, at: http://www.shemayisrael.co.il

1236 AD: Pope Gregory ordered that church leaders in England, France, Portugal, and Spain confiscate Jewish books on the first Saturday of Lent.

1259 AD: A synod of the archdiocese in Mainz ordered Jews to wear yellow badges.

1261 AD: Duke Henry III of Brabant, Belgium, stated in his will that "Jews...must be expelled from Brabant and totally annihilated so that not a single one remains, except those who are willing to trade, like all other tradesmen, without money-lending and usury."

1267 AD: The Synod of Vienna ordered Jews to wear horned hats. Thomas

Aquinas said that Jews should live in perpetual servitude. The Synod of Breslau decreed compulsory ghettos for Jews.

1279 AD: The Synod of Ofen decreed that Christians can not sell or rent real estate to Jews.

1290 AD: Jews were exiled from England and southern Italy. About 16,000 left the country.

1294 AD: Jews were expelled from Bern.

1298 AD: Jews were persecuted in Austria, Bavaria and Franconia. One hundred and forty Jewish communities were destroyed; more than 100,000 Jews were killed over a six-month period.

1298 AD: The Jews of Röttingen were charged with profaning the Host. Rindfleisch, a nobleman of that place, pretending to have received a mission from heaven to avenge this desecration and to exterminate "the accursed race of the Jews," gathered a mob around him and burned the Jews of Röttingen at the stake (April 20, 1298). Under his leadership the mob went from town to town, killing all the Jews that fell into their power, save those who accepted Christianity. The great community of Würzburg was entirely annihilated (July 24).]

Profaning the Host

Jews were frequently accused of desecrating the host (Communion bread or wafer), an accusation equal in gravity to the Catholic theology of those days as to that of desecrating relics and images of Jesus and the saints. The Jews were alleged to steal the host or to acquire it by purchase or bribery, to break it or boil it, and to stick needles into it at which point it began to bleed. Even when such an accusation was supported only by the testimony of a thief, a recent convert, or someone having a grudge against the accused Jews, the alleged perpetrators were put on trial, and, on evidence that was often preposterous, or after a confession exacted by torture, were condemned and burned, sometimes with all the other Jews of the place.

A Teacher's Guide to the Holocaust. Florida Center for

Instructional Technology, College of Education, University of South Florida, 2006.

1306 AD: One hundred thousand Jews were exiled from France. They left with only the clothes on their backs, and food for only one day.

1306 AD: One hundred thousand Jews were exiled from France. They left with only the clothes on their backs, and food for only one day.

1320 AD: Forty thousand French shepherds went to Palestine on the Shepherd Crusade. On the way, 140 Jewish communities were destroyed. "The shepherds laid siege to all the Jews who had come from all sides to take refuge... the Jews defended themselves heroically...but their resistance served no purpose, for the shepherds slaughtered a great number of the besieged Jews by smoke and by fire...The Jews, realizing that they would not escape alive, preferred to kill themselves... They chose one of their number (and) this man put some five hundred of them to death, with their consent. He then descended from the castle tower with the few Jewish children who still remained alive... They killed him by quartering. They spared the children, whom they made Catholics by baptism."

1321 AD: In Guienne, France, Jews were accused of having incited criminals to poison wells. Five thousand Jews were burned alive at the stake.

1338 AD: The councilors of Freiburg banned the performance of anti-Jewish scenes from the town's passion play because of the lethal bloody reactions against Jews that followed the performances.

1347 AD +: The Black Death originated in the Far East. China, Mongolia, India, central Asia, and southern Russia have all been suggested as the source. Mongol invaders brought it to Caffa in the Crimea (modern-day Fedodosiya). Defenders from the city later spread the disease throughout many Mediterranean ports. Rats initially carried the Black Death; their fleas spread the disease from the rats to humans. As the plague worsened, the germs spread from human to human. In five years, the death toll had reached 25 million. In England, two centuries passed before its population levels recovered from the plague. People looked around for someone to blame. They noted that a smaller percentage of Jews than Christians caught the disease. (This was undoubtedly due to Jewish sanitary and kosher dietary laws.)

Rumors circulated that Satan was protecting the Jews and that they were paying back the devil by poisoning wells used by Christians. The solution was to torture, murder and burn the Jews. "In Bavaria...12,000 Jews perished; in the small town of Erfurt, 3,000; Rue Brulée, 2,000 Jews; near Tours, an immense trench was dug, filled with blazing wood and in a single day 160 Jews were burned. In Strasberg 2,000 Jews were burned. In Maintz 6,000 were killed; in Worms, 400."

The Black Death

In the year 1348 that terrible contagion known as the Black Death, which journeyed from the East to devastate the whole of Europe, appeared at Strasbourg. Everywhere famine, floods, the inversion of the seasons, strange appearances in the sky, had been its precursors. In the Mediterranean Sea, as afterwards in the Baltic, ships were discovered drifting masterless, filled only by plague-stricken corpses. Every man dreaded, not merely the touch and the breath of his neighbor, but his very gaze, so subtle and so swift seemed the infection. In many parts of France it was computed that only two out of every twenty inhabitants were left alive. In Strasbourg sixteen thousand perished; in Avignon sixty thousand. In Paris, at one time, four or five hundred were dying in a day.

In a frenzy of terror and revenge the people fell upon the miserable Jews. They were accused of poisoning the wells, and every heart was steeled against them. Fear seemed to render all classes more ferocious, and the man who might sicken and die tomorrow found a wretched compensation in inflicting death today on the imagined authors of his danger. Toledo was supposed to be the center of an atrocious scheme by which the Jews, some after torture and some in terror of it, confessed that they had received poison for that purpose...Bishops, nobles and chief citizens held a diet at Binnefeld in Alsace, to concert measures of persecution. The deputies of Strasbourg, to their honor be it spoken, declared that nothing had been proved against the Jews. Their bishop was the most pitiless advocate of massacre. The result was a league of priests, lords, and people, to slay or banish every Jew. Some Christian, who had sought from pity or from avarice to save them, perished in the same flames. No power could stem the torrent.

The people had tasted blood; the priest had no mercy for the murderers of the Lord; the baron had debts easily discharged by the death of his creditor. At Strasbourg a monster scaffold was erected in the Jewish burial ground, and two thousand were burnt alive. At Basle all the Jews were burnt together in a wooden edifice erected for the purpose. At Spires they set their quarter in flames and perished by their own hands. A guard kept out the populace while men commissioned by the senate hunted for treasure among the smoking ruins. The corrupting bodies of those slain in the streets were put in empty wine casks and rolled into the Rhine.

When the rage for slaughter had subsided, hands, red with Hebrew blood, were piously employed in building belfries and repairing churches with Jewish tombstones and the materials of Jewish houses.

Robert Alfred Vaughn.

Hours With the Mystics (1856), 3rd ed., London, Strahan & Co., 1879, v.1, pp. 313f., 315 f.

1350 AD: Jews were expelled from many parts of Germany.

1354 AD: Twelve thousand Jews were executed in Toledo.

1367 AD: Jews were expelled from Hungary.

1374 AD: An epidemic of possession broke out in the lower Rhine region of what is now Germany. People were seen "dancing, jumping and [engaging in] wild raving." This was triggered by enthusiastic revels on St. John's Day – a Christianized version of an ancient Pagan seasonal day of celebration that was still observed by the populace. The epidemic spread throughout the Rhine and much of the Netherlands and Germany. Crowds of 500 or more dancers would be overcome together. Exorcisms were tried, but failed. Pilgrimages to the shrine of St. Vitus were tried, but this only seemed to exacerbate the problem. Finally, the rumor spread that God was angry because Christians had been excessively tolerant towards the Jews. God had cursed Europe as He did Saul when he showed mercy towards God's enemies in the Old Testament. Jews "were plundered, tortured and murdered by tens of thousands." The epidemic finally burned itself out two centuries later, in the late 16th century.

1381 AD: Jews were expelled from Strasbourg.

1391 AD: Jewish persecutions began in Seville and in 70 other Jewish communities throughout Spain.

1394 AD: Jews were exiled, for the second time, from France.

1420 AD: Jews were expelled from Mainz by the archbishop.

1421 AD: Jews were expelled from Austria.

1424 AD: Jews were expelled from Fribourg and Zurich.

1426 AD: Jews were expelled from Cologne.

1432 AD: Jews were expelled from Saxony.

1431 AD +: The Council of Basel "forbade Jews to go to universities, prohibited them from acting as agents in the conclusion of contracts between Christians, and required that they attend church sermons."

1434 AD: "Jewish men in Augsburg had to sew yellow buttons to their clothes. Across Europe, Jews were forced to wear a long undergarment, an overcoat with a yellow patch, bells and tall pointed yellow hats with a large button on them."

1453 AD: The Franciscan monk, Capistrano, persuaded the King of Poland to terminate all Jewish civil rights.

1492 AD: Jews were given the choice of being baptized as Christians or be banished from Spain. Three hundred thousand left Spain penniless. Many migrated to Turkey, where they found tolerance among the Muslims. Others converted to Christianity but often continued to practice Judaism in secret.

1497 AD: Jews were banished from Portugal. Twenty thousand left the country rather than be baptized.

1516 AD: The Governor of the Republic of Venice decided that Jews would be permitted to live only in one area of the city. It was located in the South Girolamo parish and was called the "Ghetto Novo." This was the first ghetto in Europe. Hitler made use of the concept in the 1930s.

1523 AD: Martin Luther distributed his essay, "That Jesus Was Born a Jew." He hoped that large numbers of Jews would convert to Christianity.

"That Jesus Was Born A Jew" by Martin Luther 1523

"If I had been a Jew and had seen such dolts and blockheads govern and teach the Christian faith, I would sooner have become a hog than a Christian. They have dealt with the Jews as if they were dogs rather than human beings; they have done little else than deride them and seize their property.

"When they baptize them they show them nothing of Christian doctrine or life, but only subject them to popishness and monkery....

"If the apostles, who also were Jews, had dealt with us Gentiles as we Gentiles deal with the Jews, there would never have been a Christian among the Gentiles.

"When we are inclined to boast of our position (as Christians) we should remember that we are but Gentiles, while the Jews are of the lineage of Christ. We are aliens and in-laws; they are blood relatives, cousins, and brothers of our Lord. Therefore, if one is to boast of flesh and blood the Jews are actually nearer to Christ than we are.

"If we really want to help them, we must be guided in our dealings with them not by papal law but by the law of Christian love. We must receive them cordially, and permit them to trade and work with us, that they may have occasion and opportunity to associate with us, hear our Christian teaching, and witness our Christian life.

"If some of them should prove stiff-necked, what of it? After all, we ourselves are not all good Christians either."

1540 AD: Jews were exiled from Naples.

1543 AD: Distressed by the reluctance of Jews to convert to Christianity, Martin Luther developed a hatred for Jews, as expressed in his 65,000-word treatise, "On the Jews and Their Lies." It was not until 1994 that the Lutheran Church publicly responded and repented of these abominable writings of their denominational founder, Martin Luther. In their "Declaration of the Evangelical Lutheran Church in America to the Jewish Community," April 18, 1994, they express "deep and abiding sorrow" concerning his words.

"On the Jews and Their Lies" by Martin Luther 1543

"I have come to the conclusion that the Jews will always curse and blaspheme God and his King Christ, as all the prophets have predicted....For they are thus given over by the wrath of God to reprobation, that they may become incorrigible, as Ecclesiastes says, for every one who is incorrigible is rendered worse rather than better by correction.

"...eject them forever from this country. For, as we have heard, God's anger with them is so intense that gentle mercy will only tend to make them worse and worse, while sharp mercy will reform them but little. Therefore, in any case, away with them! What then shall we Christians do with this damned, rejected race of Jews?

- "First, their synagogues or churches should be set on fire...

- "Secondly, their homes should likewise be broken down and destroyed....They ought to be put under one roof or in a stable, like Gypsies.

- "Thirdly, they should be deprived of their prayer books and Talmuds in which such idolatry, lies, cursing and blasphemy are taught.

- "Fourthly, their rabbis must be forbidden under threat of death to teach any more...

- "Fifthly, passport and traveling privileges should be absolutely forbidden to the Jews...

- "Sixthly, they ought to be stopped from usury. All their cash and valuables of silver and gold ought to be taken from them and put aside for safe keeping....

- "Seventhly, let the young and strong Jews and Jewesses be given the flail, the axe, the hoe, the spade, the distaff, and spindle and let them earn their bread by the sweat of their noses as in enjoined upon Adam's children...

"To sum up, dear princes and nobles who have Jews in your domains, if this advice of mine does not suit you, then find a better one so that you and we may all be free of this insufferable devilish burden - the Jews."

1550 AD: Jews were exiled from Genoa and Venice.

1555 AD - JUL 12: A Roman Catholic Papal bull *Cum nimis absurdum* (official letter from the Pope consisting of a formal announcement), required Jews to wear badges, and live in ghettos. They were not allowed to own property outside the ghetto. Living conditions were dreadful: over 3,000 people were forced to live in about 8 acres of land. Women had to wear a yellow veil or scarf; men had to wear a piece of yellow cloth on their hat.

1582 AD: Jews were expelled from Holland.

1648-9 AD: Bogdan Chmielnicki led an uprising against Polish rule in the Ukraine. The secondary goal of Chmielnicki and his followers was to exterminate all Jews in the country. The massacre began with the slaughter of about 6,000 Jews in Nemirov. Other major mass murders occurred in Tulchin, Polonnoye, Volhynia, Bar, Lvov, etc. Jewish records estimate that a total of 100,000 Jews were murdered and 300 communities destroyed. (Unbelievably, Chmielnicki is considered a nationalist hero in the Ukraine. In Kiev there is a large statue in the main square erected in his honor.)

Slaughter of the Jews in Russia

"On the same day 1,500 people were killed in the city of Human in Russia on the Sabbath. The nobles [Cossacks] with whom the wicked mob had again made an alliance chased all the Jews from the city into the fields and vineyards where the villains surrounded them in a circle, stripped them to their skin and ordered them to lie on the ground.

"The villains spoke to the Jews with friendly and consoling words: 'Why do you want to be killed, strangled and slaughtered like an offering to your God who poured out His anger upon you without mercy? Would it not be safer for you to worship our gods, our images and crosses and we would form one people which would unite together?'"

"But the holy and faithful people who so often allowed themselves to be murdered for the sake of the Lord, raised their voices together in almighty in Heaven and cried: 'Hear O Israel the Lord our God, the Holy One and the King of the Universe, we have been murdered for Thy sake so often already. O, Lord God of Israel let us remain faithful to Thee.'"

"Now the villains turned upon them and there was not one of them who did not fall victim."

(Account from a Lithuanian Rabbi Shabbetai ben Meir HaCohen (1621-1662) also known as the Shach, who survived this time.)

1794 AD: Jewish men were forced to serve twenty-five years in the Russian military. Many hundreds of thousands of Jews were forced to leave their homes in Russia.

1806 AD: A French Jesuit Priest, Abbe Barruel, had written a treatise blaming the Masonic Order for the French Revolution. He later issued a letter alleging that Jews, not the Masons, were the guilty party. This triggered a belief in an international Jewish conspiracy in Germany, Poland and some other European countries later in the 19th century.

1819 AD: During the late 18th and early 19th centuries, many European Jews lobbied their governments for emancipation. They sought citizenship as well as the same rights and treatment enjoyed by non-Jews. This appears to have provoked anti-Semites to engage in sporadic anti-Jewish violence. Jews and their property were attacked first in Wuerzburg, Germany during 1819 – The rioting spread across Germany, and eventually reached as far as Denmark and Poland.

1840 AD: A rumor spread in Syria that some Jews were responsible for the ritual killing of a Roman Catholic monk and his servant. As a result of horrendous treatment, some local Jews confessed to a crime they did not commit. This Damascus Affair spurred early Zionist writers like Hess to promote the Zionist cause.

1846-1878 AD: Pope Pius IX restored all the previous restrictions against the Jews within the Vatican state. All Jews under Papal control were confined to Rome's ghetto – the last one in Europe until the Nazi era restored the church's practice. (On September 3rd, 2000, Pope John Paul II beatified Pius IX [the last step before sainthood]. He explained: "Beatifying a son of the church does not celebrate particular historic choices that he has made, but rather points him out for imitation and for veneration for his virtue.")

1858 AD: Edgardo Mortara, age six, was kidnapped from his Jewish family by Roman Catholic officials after they found out that a maid had secretly baptized him. He was not returned to his family but was raised a Catholic. He eventually became a priest.

1881 AD: Alexander II of Russia was assassinated by radicals. The Jews were blamed. About 200 individual pogroms against the Jews followed. (Pogrom is a Russian word meaning devastation or riot. In Russia, a pogrom was typically a mob riot against Jewish individuals, shops, homes or businesses. They were often supported and even organized by the government.) Thousands of Jews became homeless and impoverished. The few who were charged with offenses generally received very light sentences.

Pogroms

Pogrom: an organized massacre of helpless people; specifically, a massacre of Jews.

The term "pogrom" became commonly used in English after a large-scale wave of anti-Jewish riots swept through southwestern Imperial Russia in 1881-1884. A much bloodier wave of pogroms broke out in 1903-1906, leaving an estimated 2,000 Jews dead, and many more wounded, as the Jews took to arms to defend their families and property from the attackers.

Many pogroms accompanied the Revolution of 1917 and in the ensuing Russian Civil War, an estimated 70,000 to 250,000 civilian Jews were killed in the atrocities throughout the former Russian Empire; the number of Jewish orphans exceeded 300,000. Even after the end of World War II, there were still a few pogroms in Poland, such as the Kraków pogrom on August 11, 1945 or, the infamous Kielce pogrom of 1946.

The Jewish Encyclopedia and Wissenschaft des Judentums

1893 AD: "...anti-Semitic parties won sixteen seats in the German Reichstag."

1894 AD: Captain Alfred Dreyfus, (of Jewish background), an officer on the French general staff, was convicted of treason. The evidence against him consisted of a piece of paper from his wastebasket with another person's handwriting, and papers forged by anti-Semitic officers. He received a life sentence on Devil's Island, off the coast of South America.

The French government was aware that a Major Esterhazy was actually guilty. The church, government and army united to suppress the truth. Writer Emile Zola and politician Jean Jaurès fought for justice and human rights. After ten years, the French government fell and Dreyfus was declared totally innocent. The Dreyfus Affair was world-wide news for years. It motivated journalist Theodor Herzl to write a book in 1896 entitled *The Jewish State: A Modern Solution to the Jewish Question.*

This book led to the founding of the Zionist movement that fought for a Jewish Homeland. A half-century later, the state of Israel was born.

1903 AD: At Easter, government agents organized an anti-Jewish pogrom in Kishinev, Moldova, Russia. The local newspaper published a series of inflammatory articles. A Christian child was discovered murdered and a young Christian woman at the Jewish Hospital committed suicide. Jews were blamed for the deaths. Violence ensued. The 5,000 soldiers in the town did nothing. When the smoke cleared, 49 Jews had been killed, 500 were injured; 700 homes looted and destroyed, 600 businesses and shops looted, 2,000 families left homeless. Later, it was discovered that the child had been murdered by its relatives and the suicide was unrelated to the Jews.

1905 AD: The Okhrana, the Russian secret police in the reign of Czar Nicholas II, converted an earlier anti-Semitic novel into a document called the Protocols of the Learned Elders of Zion It was published privately in 1897. A Russian Orthodox priest, Sergius Nilus, published the document publicly in 1905. It was promoted as the record of "secret rabbinical conferences whose aim was to subjugate and exterminate the Christians." The Protocols were used by the Okhrana in a propaganda campaign associated with massacres of the Jews. These were known as the Czarist Pogroms of 1905.

The Protocols of the Learned Elders of Zion

The Protocols is a plagiarized fictional book, written in an attempt to incite anti-Semitic hated. Created by "Okhrana," the Russian secret police, and first printed in 1897, it blames the Jews for all the problems in the country. Copied from a nineteenth century novel by Hermann Goedsche (Biarritz, 1886), the storyline is built around a secret Jewish sect plotting to take over the world.

The Protocols was published in 1920 in a Michigan newspaper started by Henry Ford mainly to attack Jews and Communists. Even after they were exposed as a complete forgery, Ford's paper continued to present the document as being factual.

"The only statement I care to make about the 'Protocols' is

that they fit in with what is going on. They are sixteen years old, and they have fitted the world situation up to this time. They fit it now." - Henry Ford, February 17, 1921, whose newspaper, the Dearborn Independent, cited the Protocols as evidence of an alleged Jewish threat until at least 1927.

Adolf Hitler later used the Protocols to help rationalize his assault against the Jews during World War II.

"To what extent the whole existence of this people is based on a continuous lie is shown incomparably by the 'Protocols of the Wise Men of Zion'...." - Adolf Hitler, Mein Kampf

The Protocols of the Wise Men of Zion was sold in Wal-Mart's online bookstore until September 21, 2004.

1915 AD: Six hundred thousand Jews were forcibly moved from the western borders of Russia towards the interior. About 100,000 died of exposure or starvation.

1917 AD: In the civil war following the Bolshevik Revolution of 1917, the reactionary White Armies made extensive use of the Protocols to incite widespread slaughters of Jews. Two hundred thousand Jews were murdered in the Ukraine alone.

1920 AD: The Protocols reached England and the United States. They were exposed as a forgery, but continued to be widely circulated. Henry Ford sponsored a study of international activities of Jews. This led to a series of anti-Semitic articles in the Dearborn Independent, which were published in a book, The International Jew.

1920 AD: The defeat of Germany in World War I and the continuing economic difficulties were blamed on the "Jewish influence" in that country. One anti-Semitic poster has been preserved from that era. It shows a German, presumably Christian woman, a male Jew with distorted facial features, a coffin and the word "Deutschland" (Germany).

1925 AD: Hitler published Mein Kampf, writing: "Today I believe that I am acting in accordance with the will of the Almighty Creator; by defending myself against the Jew, I am fighting for the work of the Lord."

The "Christianity" of Adolf Hitler

From his speech in Munich on April 12, 1922.

"...I say: My feelings as a Christian points me to my Lord and Savior as a fighter. It points me to the man who once in loneliness, surrounded only by a few followers, recognized these Jews for what they were and summoned men to the fight against them and who, God's truth!...was greatest not as sufferer but as fighter.

"Today, after two thousand years, with deepest emotion I recognize more profoundly than ever before – the fact that it was for this that He had to shed His blood upon the Cross. As a Christian I have no duty to allow myself to be cheated, but I have the duty to be a fighter for truth and justice. And as a man I have the duty to see to it that human society does not suffer the same catastrophic collapse as did the civilization of the ancient world some two thousand years ago – a civilization which was driven to its ruin through this same Jewish people.

"And if there is anything which could demonstrate that we are acting rightly, it is the distress which daily grows. For as a Christian I have also a duty to my own people. And when I look on my people I see it work and work and toil and labor, and at the end of the week it has only for its wage wretchedness and misery. When I go out in the morning and see these men standing in their queues and look into their pinched faces, then I believe I would be no Christian, but a very devil, if I felt no pity for them, if I did not, as did our Lord two thousand years ago, turn against those by whom today this poor people is plundered and exploited."

1930 AD: Persecution of Jews commenced in Hitler Germany, with the inception of the systematic destruction of 6 million Jews (including 1.5 million children) throughout Nazi-occupied Europe.

1933 AD: Hitler became chancellor in Germany. On April 1, Julius

Streicher organized a one-day boycott of all Jewish owned business in the country. This was the start of continuous oppression by the Nazis culminating in the Holocaust (a.k.a. *Shoah*). Jews "were barred from civil service, legal professions and universities, were not allowed to teach in schools and could not be editors of newspapers." Two years later, Jews were no longer considered citizens.

1934 AD: Various laws were enacted in Germany to force Jews out of schools and professions.

1935 AD: The Nazis passed the Nuremberg Laws restricting citizenship to those of "German or related blood." Jews became stateless.

1936 AD: Cardinal Hloud of Poland urged Catholics to boycott all Jewish businesses.

1938 AD: On November 9, the Nazi government in Germany sent storm troopers, the SS and the Hitler Youth on a pogrom that killed 91 Jews, injured hundreds, burned 177 synagogues and looted 7,500 Jewish stores. Broken glass could be seen everywhere, resulting in this event becoming known as Kristallnacht, the Night of Broken Glass.

Kristallnacht

The Germans had been looking for a way to get rid of their Jews. They decided the Polish Jews would be first so they were rounded up on the cold, rainy night of October 28, and 17,000 Polish Jews were beaten across the border into Poland.

A 17-year-old Polish Jew who was living in Paris named Henry Grynspan had parents who were part of the German-forced, Jewish exile. This brave young man felt the need to show the world what was happening to the Jews in Germany. Acquiring a gun, he walked into the German Embassy in Paris and shot the first man he saw – an embassy official named Ernst Von Rath. Von Rath died, and this triggered a "spontaneous" uprising against the Jews. (The furor had actually been planned for some time – this event was the pretext to put the plan into action.)

"On the nights of November 9 and 10, gangs of Nazi youth roamed through Jewish neighborhoods breaking windows of Jewish businesses and homes, burning synagogues and looting. In all 101 synagogues were destroyed and almost 7,500 Jewish businesses were destroyed. 26,000 Jews were arrested and sent to concentration camps, Jews were physically attacked and beaten and 91 died." (Snyder, Louis L. *Encyclopedia of the Third Reich*. New York: Paragon House, 1989:201).

Three days later, on November 12, a meeting was called, which included the top Nazi leadership, to assess the damage done during the night and place responsibility for it.

"It was decided at the meeting that, since Jews were to blame for these events, they be held legally and financially responsible for the damages incurred by the pogrom. Accordingly, a 'fine of one billion marks was levied for the slaying of Von Rath, and six million marks paid by insurance companies for broken windows was to be given to the state coffers.'" (Snyder, Louis L. *Encyclopedia of the Third Reich*. New York: Paragon House, 1989:201).

Kristallnacht turned out to be a crucial turning point in German strategy regarding the Jews and is considered by many as the actual beginning of the Holocaust.

1938 AD: Hitler brought back century-old church law, ordering all Jews to wear a yellow Star of David as identification. A few hundred thousand Jews were allowed to leave Germany after they gave all their assets to the government.

1939 AD: The Holocaust, the Shoah – the systematic extermination of Jews in Germany – begins. The process only ended in 1945 with the conclusion of World War II. Approximately 6 million Jews (1.5 million of them children), 400 thousand Roma (Gypsies) and others were slaughtered. Some were killed by death squads; others were slowly killed in trucks with carbon monoxide; others were gassed in large groups in Auschwitz, Dachau, Sobibor, Treblinka and other extermination camps. Officially, the Holocaust was described by the Nazis as subjecting Jews "to special treatment" or as a "solution of the Jewish question." Gold taken from the teeth of the victims was recycled; hair was used in the manufacture of mattresses.

1939 AD: The St. Louis, a German luxury cruise ship, crammed with 906 German Jewish refugees escaping the Nazi threat arrived in the Havana harbor and was denied the right to dock in Cuba. Days later, the U.S. immigration office refused the St. Louis permission to dock in Florida and enter our nation. The ship was forced to return to Germany where certain death awaited most of the refugees.

Voyage of the St. Louis

Sailing so close to Florida that they could see the lights of Miami, passengers on the "St. Louis" cabled President Franklin D. Roosevelt asking for refuge.

Roosevelt never answered the cable.

The State Department and the White House had already decided not to let them enter the United States. A State Department telegram sent to a passenger stated that the passengers must "await their turns on the waiting list and then qualify for and obtain immigration visas before they may be admissible into the United States."

Visas could have been granted to the passengers only by denying them to the thousands of German Jews who had already applied for them. President Roosevelt could have issued an executive order to admit additional refugees, but chose not to do so for a variety of political reasons.

United States Holocaust Memorial Museum, Washington, D.C. Encyclopedia

1940 AD: The Vichy government of France collaborated with Nazi Germany by freezing about 80,000 Jewish bank accounts. During the next four years, they deported about 76,000 Jews to Nazi death camps; only about 2,500 survived. It was only in

1995 that French President Jacques Chirac "was able to admit that the state bore a heavy share of responsibility in the mass round-ups and deportations of Jews, as well as in the property and asset seizures that were carried out with the active help of the Vichy regime."

1941 AD: The Holocaust Museum in Washington, DC, estimates that 13,000 Jews died on June 19, 1941, during a pogrom in Bucharest, Romania. It was ordered by the pro-Nazi Romanian regime of Marshal Ion Antonescu. The current Romanian government has admitted that this atrocity happened, but most Romanians continue to deny that the Jews were killed on orders from their own government.

1941 AD: Polish citizens in Jedwabne in northeastern Poland killed hundreds of Jews, by either beating them to death or burning them alive in a barn. According to the Associated Press: "The role played by Polish citizens was suppressed for nearly six decades until publication of a book by a Polish émigré historian, Jan Tomasz Gross. After release of the book in 2000, the Polish government launched an investigation. 'The role of the Poles was decisive in conducting the criminal act,' [prosecutor Radoslaw] Ignatiew, said. The book, *Neighbours,*sparked national soul-searching among Poles, many of whom could not believe that anybody but the Nazis would have committed the atrocity."

1942 AD: At the Wannsee conference, the Nazi leaders of Germany, decided on "the final solution of the Jewish question," which was the attempt to exterminate every Jew in Europe. From July 28 to 31, almost 18,000 Russian inhabitants of the Minsk ghetto in what is now Belarus were exterminated. This in addition to 5,000 to 15,000 who had been massacred in earlier pogroms in that city. This was just one of many such pogroms during World War II.

1945 AD: The Holocaust ended as the Allied Forces overran the Nazi death camps.

1946 AD: Even though World War II ended the year before, anti-Semitic pogroms continued, particularly in Poland, with the deaths of many Jews.

C3CR8O8O

I end the history of persecution of Jews by Christians, at the end of WWII but, tragically, not because the end of the Holocaust was the end of the Jewish persecution by Christians.

Simply read former president Jimmy Carter's *Palestine: Peace, Not Apartheid,* and be reminded that Christian anti-Semitism is still very much alive and unwell.

Answering the Question

Rabbi Isaac faintly smiled and asked again, "Does the Christian community have the patience for us?"

My answer at the time was, "Rabbi, we are not waiting for anything. There is no need for patience on our part concerning the Jewish people."

Since the time of this workshop I have had many opportunities to reconsider Rabbi Isaac's fears about the new Christian Zionist support.

The Jews feel a solidarity with their past, as if they are all on the same train. Throughout history, Christian societies have derailed the Jewish train, over and over again. Christians generally sense no such relationship or connection with our history. Most don't even know there is "a train."

This ponderous question concerning "Christian patience" should reverberate with an overwhelming and searing conviction if we allow ourselves to embrace even the slightest amount of culpability in light of our Christian history with the Jewish people.

Only until we are willing to step into the insane hopelessness of being on the Jewish side of this horrendous experience, only until we imagine being maligned and cursed for 1,900 years as the assassins of the Christian Jesus, only until we envision our own wife/husband, brother, sister, mother, father or child bound to the burning stakes of the Christian Inquisition, only until we have allowed ourselves to feel our 14-year-old daughter ripped from our arms and shoved into a parade of beautiful children who will be raped by ravenous Nazi officer pedophiles in the "Christian" nation of Germany...it is only until then, we might begin to understand the true horror of the rabbi's question.

How disoriented, how battered the historic Christian curse has left the Jewish people in their dealings with our faith.

Even with the blessed bounty of their God-given brilliance and resilience, they have been forced into a coma of self-preservation when trying to reconcile this new Christian love for them with the history of those who also carried the cross.

"Does the Christian community have the patience for us?"

Is the answer not appallingly evident? It is we Christians, with broken hearts and bowed heads who must beseech every Jew we have the privilege of knowing: "Does the Jewish community have the patience for us?"

Question 2

"Do Christians still hate us because we don't believe in Jesus?"

Standard Christian Answer:
"Hate you? We don't hate you. How did you ever get such a crazy idea that we hated you? We love you and want you to know that..." and the "Jesus talk" begins.

The Founders Group

The Founders Group is composed of a select number of prominent citizens, each the founder of a successful business. The group offers both social and substantive opportunities to meet people who can play a role in shaping the Jewish community and the wider world. This group is energetic and creative.

Guest speakers at the philanthropy meetings have included: Senator Joseph Lieberman, Dr. Henry Kissinger, Prime Minister Ehud Barak, Steven Spielberg, Dr. Charles Krauthammer, Congressman Eric Cantor, Irshad Manji (author of *The Trouble with Islam*), Hala Mustafa (a leader of Arab reform), Martin Kramer (author of *Ivory Towers on Sand*), and other prominent philanthropists, political figures, and scholars.

I had just finished my presentation to the group when a Jewish woman startled me by asking, "Do you still hate us because we don't believe in Jesus?"

I was stunned, and for a moment speechless.

"What?" I hesitated, in disbelief. "Do we still hate you?"

Unable to grasp the question, I continued, "Do you actually think that there are Christians today who hate you because you don't believe what we believe about Jesus?"

Her immediate response was a guarded, nervous nod of her head followed by a whispered, "Well, yes." In dismay I quickly locked eyes with the two Jewish men standing next to her and inquired, "Is this something you've ever believed? That Christians actually hate you because you don't believe in Jesus?"

"Sure," they both answered, as nonchalantly as if I had asked, "Would you like to go grab a sandwich?"

Tears filled my eyes and trickled down my cheeks. "I am so sorry," I offered them.

Why Would Jews Believe Christians Hate Them?

The question is not often presented to me quite as directly or with such sincerity, but it is a question many Jews ponder. Christians must deeply consider why it remains a question to Jews and when asked, answer with the understanding and humility such a question demands.

Immediately after this occurrence, I asked my Jewish buddy David Brog, the Executive Director of Christians United for Israel (CUFI), if this was a genuine concern on the hearts of the Jewish community.[1] I had been active as a Christian Zionist for over two decades, and neither the thought nor the actual question had ever crossed my mind or been asked with such transparency.

"Well, Victor," David began with a wry smile, signifying that he was getting ready both to educate me and boot me across the room

---

[1] David Brog is a conservative Jew serving as Executive Director of Christians United for Israel (CUFI). David lives and writes in Washington, DC, and worked in the United States Senate for seven years, rising to be chief of staff to a senior United States senator and staff director of the Senate Judiciary Committee. Prior to his time on Capitol Hill, David practiced corporate law in Tel Aviv, Israel and Philadelphia, Pennsylvania. David is a graduate of Princeton University and Harvard Law School. He is the author of *Standing With Israel, Why Christians Support The Jewish State.* I pray that this book become required reading in all of our Christian seminary campuses. I implore you, as well, to read it.

like a soccer ball. "If you remember, you guys hunted us down and killed us for quite a few years because we didn't believe what you did about Jesus. So, for a lot of Jews, yeah... that kind of left us with the impression you don't like us much," he explained.

"Well, when you say it like that..." I almost answered.

But I suddenly realized, for Jews it *is* like that.

For my Christian Readers:

Our Christian history in relationship to the Jewish people is one of vicious, bloody betrayal. Labeled as "Christ killers" by some of our early church "fathers," the Jews have been subjected to lethal and near perpetual Christian anti-Semitism which continues in various forms to this very day.

A Story About My Father

Before suggesting how Christians answer this question, I need you to know my remarkable father and about an event that changed his life...and mine.

My dad, Alfred Miroslav Bohumil Styrsky, loved my precious mom, his children, his God and just about every single life form upon our planet. He was enamored with the heavens, the stars, and I'm sure he would have loved extraterrestrials had he ever met one. He did not love injustice, war, bigotry, or religious arrogance of any kind.

I actually look a lot like my dad and cannot help but think about him as I see him looking back at me in the mirror every day! When loving my own children and grandchildren, I try my best to emulate the cosmic father he was to me.

For Father's Day, 1987, I wrote the following song in Dad's honor. I hope it will help you understand his influence on my life.

My Friend, My Father, My Dad

I can remember so many adventures in life with my father.

And when I was little, it all was so simple 'cause I have the best dad ever.

And now that I'm older, he still hasn't changed;
There's nobody else like that man!
My friend, my father, my dad.

I learned from him how to fish and to swim and to say, *"I'm sorry."*
We'd travel through time, as I'd climb on his knee
and he'd tell me all his stories.
And I learned from him that a man can cry,
and giving means all that you have.
My friend, my father, my dad.

Remember his words...stay on the path
 He taught you from your youth,
for it will keep you.

Now I'm a father and it sure is harder to lead than to follow.
And yet there are times when I still hear my Dad's voice inside
telling me where to go.

And when I see Jesus, I may be surprised –
He reminds me so much of that man!

My friend, my father, my dad.

© V. Styrsky 1987

My Lutheran Upbringing

Until my early teens, I accompanied my dad and mom to church out of love and respect for them. Though raised in a Christian home, I did not come to faith until I was twenty years old. The memories of my childhood church experiences are best summarized by saying, "I pretty much detested the whole thing."

- The sermons – hated them.
- The Sunday clothes I was straitjacketed into – hated them.
- The circus organ music – yuck.
- The liturgy – snore, the "lethargy"!

Ah, the liturgy:

"I believe in God, the Father Almighty, Creator of heaven and earth. I believe in Jesus Christ, His only Son, our Lord. He was conceived by the power of the Holy Spirit and born of the Virgin Mary. He suffered under Pontius Pilot, was crucified, died, and was buried."

What in the world was Jesus doing, "suffering under an *unconscious pilot*"?

The Lutheran liturgy I suffered as a child added nothing but confusion to my Sunday morning religious detention. I could not for the life of me figure out the image I had of Jesus gazing upon a pilot who had been knocked unconscious in a P-51 Mustang airplane, which apparently had crashed into a tree!

Suffered under an *unconscious pilot*?? I didn't get it.

I even remember the smell of the church, and I didn't like that, either. It was not the sweet, exciting and exotic aroma of incense, but the stale, musky smell of acute dullness.

I especially did not like the awkward and forced obligation of standing in line at the end of every service to shake hands with the stranger in a satin robe who had been preaching. This was the same man who, for the previous hour, had attempted over and over again to kill me with boredom. What in the world were my parents doing, making me shake his hand?!

These memories are my childhood religious recollections mixed with the unspoken madness inherent in the confusion of worshiping somebody I could not see or understand.

But worshiping my dad was easy, and he was easy to understand – and I did worship him.

One of my very earliest memories of life entails explaining to my 3- and 4-year-old friends in Green Bay, Wisconsin, that my dad was the very first man on the earth. My dad was Adam. He really was – to me.

My dad's accomplishments and his unconditional love for me merited his sacred position in my eyes. My dad was also a highly decorated P-51 Mustang fighter pilot during WWII. Enjoy here a page of excerpts from his personal journal briefly describing several of his missions.

Alfred Miroslav Bohumil Styrsky
(And his mascot "Flak")

BRANCH OF SERVICE
U.S. Army Air Forces
HOMETOWN: Chicago, IL
P-51 MUSTANG FIGHTER PILOT IN THE 356TH FIGHTER
SQUADRON, 354TH FIGHTER GROUP. FLEW 85 MISSIONS
OVER FRANCE AND GERMANY.
POSTHUMOUSLY AWARDED THE DISTINGUISHED FLYING
CROSS IN 2004 FOR HIS MISSION ON JANUARY 30, 1944,
OVER HANOVER, GERMANY.

England – The 354th Fighter Group:

In November 1943, a dozen of my comrades and I arrived in England as pilot replacements to be joined to the well-established 354th Fighter Group based at Boxted. We were most fortunate to be placed in such a well- trained and outstanding group of flyers.

On the 4th of July, the 356th was chosen to escort "Stars Look Down," carrying General Eisenhower and General "Pete" Quesada. While at cruising altitude I felt a hit from ground fire. I knew my plane was hit in the engine area and any moment I expected to see coolant boiling out. Keeping my eye on the gauges I worried for a while. All appeared to be okay and I continued with the mission. No one else experienced any ground fire. Later my crew chief pointed out the marksmanship of the Jerry gunner. He must have had some eye. The hole in the engine cowling was ever so near to a vital coolant line.

The modified P-51B Mustang General Eisenhower and General Elwood "Pete" Quesada used to fly a personal reconnaissance of the Saint-Lo area.

The news account of our harrowing mission on D-Day is enclosed. We escorted slow flying C-47s towing gliders, under a two thousand foot ceiling, during darkness, with no lights in snug formation. Returning fighters from the invasion area added an additional touch of suspense. To further complicate matters my engine began overheating. I found that I was able to keep the temperature normal by using the manual switch although I was taking a chance that there might have been a small coolant leak. It worked out that I was able to complete that mission.

By the end of October I had flown 84 combat missions and was placed on the list for rotation to the United States. This curtailed my combat flying. Being restless, I asked Operations (either Bob Brooks or Harry Fisk) to fly another mission. They were reluctant but finally relented and scheduled me for a dive-bombing mission of a railroad terminal. The cloudy weather hindered our mission severely. A break in the clouds made it possible to bomb the rail yard, but only one plane at a time, limited as we were by visibility restriction.

In November, my departure time came. I bid a fond good-bye to my comrades whose wings and tails I had faithfully covered through many an ordeal. I had clung to their wings flying through thousands of feet of foul weather, caught heavy flak over the Rurh Industrial Space, had ground fire lace through our formations (at times the shells looking like snowballs, a strange and hard to believe phenomenon, usually occurring on a dive bombing run), our mortal bodies hurtling through a melee of planes, protecting my lead pilots' tails as they cavorted after a bandit.

All of us drank of this cup of peril. To paraphrase a line from our Air Corps song, "How we lived? God only knew."

When I parted company of my ground crew and flying comrades that I had known for the past year it was with mixed emotions. Glad to be going home and sad to be leaving *these good friends. As Robert Brooks bid me good-bye, he told me that I would be submitted for a Distinguished Flying Cross.*

The Betrayal of My Father

Within these most condensed of observations, I hope you can capture the essence of my remarkable father. I have opened this door of my heart to you so that you may more fully comprehend one final and perplexing story about his life.

This story is not one of bravery and valor but an account of betrayal he suffered through the actions of the US Air Force. It was a betrayal that would play a critical part in ending his life and changing mine in an amazing and wonderful way.

> ***Operation Greenhouse:***
>
> *In 1951, Dad participated in the top-secret project, Operation Greenhouse, involving atomic weapon tests on Eniwetok, an island in the South Pacific; he recounts: "The first nuclear detonation was scheduled for April 8th, 1951. Volunteers were called for to fly an Air Force officer over the blast site for him to monitor the extent of radiation and pick up exposed film badges. I was chosen for the first shot, the flight to be made less than an hour after the blast. At the request of the monitor, I guided the plane right over the crater site at which point the monitor, alarmed by the sudden extreme readings on his hand-held radiation counter, shouted, 'Get us out of here!'"*

My father writes, "At no time were we advised of the cumulative radiation exposure we had taken on our person."

The United States Air Force buried my father's medical record, which noted the dangerous, and eventually deadly dose of radiation to which he had been exposed. They immediately removed him from Operation Greenhouse and sent him home, telling him that he should suffer no ill effects from the mission, other than being sterile.

The family joke is that I was born almost exactly nine months from the day he came home to my mom. Realizing I am the fruit of radioactive spermizoid has been very helpful to my friends and family as they try to understand me.

My father's health was gravely affected by this incident. Had he been informed of the deadly radiation dosage to which he had been exposed, there were medical procedures and precautions that could have benefited his life to a great extent. As it was, he suffered enormously because of the deceitful actions of the institution he trusted and courageously served. The institution that should have protected and honored my father had betrayed him.

A Life-Changing Confession and Apology

One day, before my dad passed away, he received a letter from a young officer in the United States Air Force. This honorable young man was not even alive during the Second World War but upon discovering the hidden medical records concerning this event at Eniwetok, he wrote an apology to my father. In the letter, he attempted to confess the "sins" that the US Air Force had committed against Dad (using military jargon, of course) and to ask him and our family for forgiveness.

My father was such a good and forgiving man and had never sought after this confession; yet the unexpected letter's content greatly uplifted his spirit.

This admission by the United States Air Force of their transgression against my father, and their recognition of the unjust suffering he endured as a result touched me in a very profound way. As far as I am concerned, the US Air Force has not done anything as righteous in its entire existence. How could I feel anything less?

The military's apology, although withheld for over 40 years, somehow helped mend my personal wounds of grief and injustice concerning the matter.

The Lack of Christian Culpability

Just as the officer who wrote to my father identified with the failures of his military community members who served a generation before him, so the Hebrew prophet Nehemiah identified with, and sought forgiveness for, the sins of the Israelites from the generation past.

Nehemiah 1:6-7:

> I confess the sins we Israelites, including myself and my father's house, have committed against you. We have acted very wickedly toward you. We have not obeyed the commands, decrees and laws you gave your servant Moses.

In an account recorded in the book of 2 Samuel 21, we find God requiring confession of sin and restitution from King David for the sins of a previous generation:

> There was a famine during David's reign that lasted for three years, so David asked the Lord about it. And the Lord said, "The famine has come because Saul and his family are guilty of murdering the Gibeonites."
>
> So the king summoned the Gibeonites. They were not part of Israel but were all that was left of the nation of the Amorites. The people of Israel had sworn not to kill them, but Saul, in his zeal for Israel and Judah, had tried to wipe them out.
>
> David asked them, "What can I do for you? How can I make amends so that you will bless the Lord's people again?"
>
> "Well, money can't settle this matter between us and the family of Saul," the Gibeonites replied. "Neither can we demand the life of anyone in Israel."
>
> "What can I do then?" David asked. "Just tell me and I will do it for you."
>
> Then they replied, "It was Saul who planned to destroy us, to keep us from having any place at all in the territory of Israel. So let seven of Saul's sons be handed over to us, and we will execute them before the Lord at Gibeon, on the mountain of the Lord."

"All right," the king said, "I will do it."

...The men of Gibeon executed them on the mountain before the Lord. So all seven of them died together at the beginning of the barley harvest. Then the king ordered that they bury the bones in the tomb of Kish, Saul's father, at the town of Zela in the land of Benjamin. After that, God ended the famine in the land.

How can we Christians today explain doing anything less than identifying with the sins of our past generations toward the Jewish people?

Though we were not present during the Crusades or the Inquisition, it is very doubtful that we would have fought against the Christian insanity of those times. During the time of Martin Luther, in all probability we would have followed in lockstep behind his anti-Semitic theology, as did the mesmerized Hitler Youth behind the lethal wake of Adolf Hitler.

We can begin to make amends today for what was done then.

Though we almost certainly would have joined mute voices with the deadly silent church choir during the horrors of the Shoah, we can today resolve to stand up and speak out in opposition to the anti-Semitic war being waged against the Jewish people.

For my Christian readers:

Holocaust is from the Greek *holokauston* meaning "burnt whole" or "that which is completely burnt" and refers to Hitler's genocide of 6 million Jews (almost 2/3 of the European Jewish population). The Hebrew *Shoah* meaning "total and tragic annihilation that surpassed everything" is the term used by many Jews when speaking of this unspeakably wicked moment in history as it more accurately describes the devastation caused by it.

Understanding the Question

We will not wholly understand or know the pain of another unless we have experienced the same suffering. The most empathetic observer is still incapable of fully comprehending the intimate effects of an affliction upon the one enduring it.

Through the circumstance in my father's life, and through the confession of a young, gallant and godly officer serving in the US Air Force, I have tasted a portion of the unjust suffering as well as the worthy vindication of my dad.

His hardship and the repentance of the US Air Force are, of course, in no way proportionate to the affliction of the Jewish people and the need of repentance from the Christian community, but this very personal experience changed my life.

Until these events had touched our family, I had never considered how appalling it is for a Jew to be lunged at with a Jesus pamphlet by a Christian stranger claiming "love" for him. I believe I am beginning to understand how we provoke the Jews' disdain from our mechanical missionary attempts that have so little to do with the love of Jesus.

Unless we embrace the appalling historic suffering the Jewish people have endured from those who have claimed faith in Christ, we can never begin to comprehend the Jewish justified dismay with our unsolicited attempts to witness to them.

In the spirit of this understanding, I pray that the efforts of Christian Zionists may begin a new history of support, encouragement and blessing to the hearts of our Jewish friends.

(If my analogy and conclusions seem harsh to my Christian brethren, I ask you to present these thoughts to your Jewish friends for their perspective. I believe they will confirm my thoughts. If you have no Jewish friends, then please keep reading this book!)

Answering the question:
"Do Christians still hate us because we don't believe in Jesus?"

I pray more and more Christians will search out and understand why this ominous question would weigh upon a Jewish heart.

I pray that the zealous Christian community begins to realize just how surreal we appear when preaching to rather than compassionately listening to the people who have been decimated under our banner for the last 1,900 years.

Consider answering the question using the thoughts within the following response:

"The abominable sins that have been committed against you over the last 1,900 years from those calling themselves Christians are the most wicked in the history of mankind. There is no restitution we can offer that could ever begin to compensate for our crimes against you and I ask God and you for forgiveness."

You must understand that this moment may be awkward. Very few Christians have ever asked Jews for forgiveness. We have chosen to keep the records of our culpability ignorantly buried or ignored, and have remained unrighteously indifferent to our Christian sins against them.

Your startled Jewish inquirer will possibly try to explain to you that his concept of forgiveness does not really work in this manner. In an inexplicable way however, I believe he has granted your request immediately upon hearing your words. Thank him and then finish answering the question:

"Of course we don't hate you. We believe that you are the beloved of HaShem and the apple of His eye, and I bless you in the name of the God of Abraham, Isaac, and Jacob."

For my Christian readers:

"The living cannot forgive on behalf of the dead."

Question 3

"What is your real agenda in reaching out to the Jews?"

Standard Christian Answer:
"Well, we just love the Jewish people and want to help them understand that..." and the Jesus talk begins.

During a Sunday afternoon seminar hosted by "NEVER AGAIN – Christians Standing With Israel," in the Q & A session a middle-aged Christian woman asked our distinguished Jewish guest speaker, "How does it make you guys feel knowing that the only reason Christians are helping you is to bring you to believe in Jesus?"

Her statement was sadly similar to the common response given by Christians when asked, "What is your real agenda in reaching out to the Jews?"

For my Christian readers:

NEVER AGAIN – Christians Standing With Israel is a Sacramento-based initiative headed by Randy Neal, the CUFI Western States Coordinator. After the Holocaust and following the birth of the nation of Israel, Jews cried out, "NEVER AGAIN! Never again will we live in the fear of being hunted down and killed. Never again, never again!" As Christian

> Zionists, we stand with the Jewish people to assure them that never again will they stand alone to face the terror of anti-Semitism.

Christian *Mashugenas*...we have more than our share

We describe these types of incidents as having a very high cringe factor, especially in light of the clear announcement at the commencement of all our events that we have a non-conversionary agenda. We have much work ahead of us to educate the Christian masses on expressing unconditional love for the Jewish people.

This biblically commanded love is an act of adoration and obedience to God, and is a blessing and a *Kiddush Hashem* for us to perform! This well-meaning woman had not yet graduated from our makeshift academy...or possibly arrived late and missed our mission statement, was hard of hearing, or is just one of the legions of unaware mashugenas in our faith community.

Our guest speaker caught the knuckleball question she flung at his heart and, without a blink, set it down with the tenderness of a father tucking his little child into bed.

God bless the Jews for their enormous longsuffering with us.

For my Christian readers:

Mashugena is Yiddish for "crazy" or "goofball"!
Kiddush HaShem is Hebrew for "sanctification of the name of God."

Getting the Jews Back to Israel – a Jewish urban myth

I was once on the phone with the personal assistant to Mayor Willie Brown during his long reign over San Francisco politics. The woman was an active pro-Israel Jewish zealot and had recently become a friend through my work with pro-Israel Christians.

"You really should publish a paper on Christian theology involving your relationship to the Jewish people," my new ally suggested.

"What exactly do you recommend it would cover?" I asked.

"Well, you know that most Jews believe that the only reason Christians are wanting to stand with us is to get us to make *aliyah* so that Jesus can return," she remarked matter-of-factly.

For my Christian readers:

Aliyah, which literally means "going up," is the Jewish legal right of return to the land of Israel.

"Wait a minute," I asked, trying to replay the answer she had just given me.

"You think we believe that we have to get the Jews to Israel so that Jesus can return?" I clumsily restated her question. The connection of those two thoughts was absolutely alien to me, thus my stumbling attempt to reiterate them. Even though I had been an active pro-Israel Christian for many years, this was the very first time I had ever been let in on this secret information concerning my real interest in the Jewish people.

Since this discovery, I have addressed many Jewish audiences of all ages and have been completely shocked to find that this belief amongst the Jewish people is held as supreme truth. Whenever I ask my Jewish friends where they first heard this story, they always answer, "From a Jew."

The reason Jews have only heard this story from other Jews is because it is nowhere to be found in Christian theology.

Let me briefly explain.

The May 14, 1948, miracle rebirth of the nation of Israel does have "Messianic Age" implications for evangelical Christians – just as it does for many Jews.

"During the ingathering of the exiles to Israel, a short time before the future Final Redemption, 'the heavens and earth will shake' (Chagai 2:6); 'This is a hint of the upheaval and confusion throughout the world. And in this place, the Land of Israel, I will give peace,' says the Lord of Hosts."
The Abarbanel, Mashmiya Yishuah, Mivaser 13.[2]

Evangelicals have no eschatological teaching (End of Days theology) that requires all Jews to be back in the land of Israel for a Messianic visitation. Neither do evangelical Christians believe that there is anything we can do to hasten the return (or first visit, as my Jewish friends believe) of Messiah.

Evangelical Christian theology concerning the coming of Messiah is fairly unified on the following points:

1) A date for the event has already been secured.
2) Only God the Father knows the time.
3) The coming of Messiah is imminent.

Mark 13:31-33:

"Heaven and earth will pass away, but My words will not pass away.

"But of that day or hour no one knows, not even the angels in heaven, nor the Son, but the Father alone. Take heed; keep on the alert, for you do not know when the appointed time will come."

This appointed time cannot and will not be hastened nor detained by our activities or lack thereof. A day has already been set and most evangelical Christians believe that the appearance of Christ is imminent.

---

[2] Rabbi Yitzchak Abarbanel 1437-1508, is known simply as "the Abarbanel." A descendant of the House of King David, he is among the most revered of Jewish Bible commentators and thinkers.

The early church believed the coming of Messiah was close at hand:

Philippians 4:4-5:

Always be full of joy in the Lord. I say it again – rejoice!
Let everyone see that you are considerate in all you do.
Remember, the Lord is coming soon.

A Night to Honor Israel

As the California Director for Christians United for Israel (CUFI), my responsibilities include gathering California Christian supporters of Israel and assisting them in hosting events called A Night to Honor Israel in their cities. From the inception of CUFI in February 2006, to the time of the writing of this book, we have held over 85 events in cities across the United States. From the Detroit, Michigan Night to Honor Israel, which was a gathering of over 6,500 people, to the Berkeley, California, celebration (yes, we held a Night to Honor Israel in Berkeley!), over $40 million has been collected. Through partnering with the local Jewish leadership of each host city, every dollar received in the evening's offering is sent to provide critical aid to Jewish recipients in the land of Israel.

The fundraising aspect of CUFI is secondary to the opportunities of creating new relationships between the members of local Jewish and Christian communities. I have been the recipient of many precious Jewish friendships because of my affiliation with CUFI, and an especially dear friend is my buddy, Avi.

Avraham (Avi) Alpert is the extremely gifted cantor of Sacramento's Mosaic Law Congregation, a constituent of the United Synagogue of Conservative Judaism.

Avi loves the Torah; he loves the God of Abraham, Isaac, and Jacob; and he loves the challenges of being an observant Jew. From his point of view, devoted dedication is not negotiable in his book or in the Torah.

I love Avi like a brother.

Avi and I first met after the Sacramento Night to Honor Israel that CUFI hosted in 2006. He had been asked to sing the national anthem, and I was honored to be the MC for the evening. Our music ministry, Wild Branches, participated in the event as well.

The Sacramento Crest Theatre was packed with close to a thousand guests from the Jewish and Christian communities. We were all treated to an extraordinary outpouring of the Spirit of God; for almost three hours we laughed, cried, sang, and even danced in the aisles during this holy convocation. Avi and I embraced at the conclusion of the evening. We both agreed that we needed to get together for coffee in the very near future.

Avi writes an article for his synagogue's monthly newsletter, *The Scroll*, which follows. I ask that you explore his thoughts concerning the effect our Sacramento Night to Honor Israel had upon his life.

Mosaic Law's November Scroll from the Cantor's Voice:

EMOTIONAL SINGING

Can singing the Star Spangled Banner be a life-changing experience? Everyone knows the words and sings along. Most Americans probably have this anthem committed to memory. Yet it is a tremendous honor to be asked to lead such a song. I recently accepted an invitation to sing our national anthem at the Crest Theatre. It was the kickoff to an evening entitled a Night to Honor Israel by CUFI (Christians United for Israel). This sold-out event and all of its sincere emotional singing and presentations unexpectedly kept tears streaming down my cheeks. After singing "and the home of the brave," I slowly began to realize how monumental it was to be legitimized as an observant Jew and as a member of the kley ko-desh *the Jewish clergy, by religious Christians.*

Last year, Rabbi Toaff told us the story of the Chief Rabbi of Rome who was invited by the Pope to the Vatican and turned down the invitation as it was during Shemini Atseret. *The Chief Rabbi would be observing God's* commandment in the Torah to abstain from creative work on the holiday. Our rabbi reminded us that not so long ago, if a rabbi or any Jew was asked to go to the Vatican, they went (for fear of their life). We live in a different world today. Christians: Catholics, Protestants, and especially Evangelicals treat Jews with honor.

While sitting at the CUFI event, listening to music and speeches that were orchestrated in an utmost respectful manner, I shed tears. These Christians proved with their voices and their videos that they want nothing more than to bless God's Chosen People. They are truly pained by the past atrocities perpetrated against Jews in the name of Christianity. They acknowledge our relationship with Hashem and want only to support us, and our State of Israel.

These are wonderful times. Jews who practice Judaism are being supported by Christians. Faith groups are feeling less threatened by others and are more willing to see value beyond their own. Members of the clergy are reaching out to colleagues who believe differently, teaching love and singing together. I pray that all of the religions of the world will begin to bless the Jews and bless the tiny State of Israel. Let us all make music of thanksgiving together.

– *Hazzan Avraham Alpert* cantor@mosaiclaw.org

Jew and Gentile Friendship

Starbucks has become a universal, neutral location for many first dates and business propositions. On October 5, 2006, Avi and I were about to experience both. I arrived fifteen minutes late and spotted him sitting outside sporting a fedora and a suit coat, looking like a million bucks. Wearing my stock California-pastor-jeans-and-T-shirt, running shoes (sans socks), and enough gel in my hair to withstand a gale, I realized I had probably underdressed for the occasion and felt like a "Cinderfella" who never got the dress code memo for the ball.

Avi got up to greet me. As soon as we both sat down, I found my new acquaintance had a lot on his mind. His heart was bursting with a recent discovery he had made, and his zeal to enlighten me was burning a hole in his spirit and thoughts.

"I've been reading a very interesting book, Pastor Styrsky," Avi formally announced. "It's written by an evangelical Christian and is called, *Misquoting Jesus*. Have you ever heard of it?" he asked.

"I haven't," I answered. But by the name of the book I assumed it was one of hundreds released every few years purporting to have the real goods on Jesus or the secret location of his first pair of sandals.

Avi let me know in no uncertain terms that the New Testament was (using his words) "a bunch of malarkey!" He explained to me his belief that the Greek documents claiming to contain the words of Christ are filled with more errors, additions, and subtractions than there are words in that entire document! (This is a belief that my buddy Avi continues to hold.)

I listened intently and loved every word Avi shared with me. "Now here is a guy with some chutzpah!" I smiled to myself.

For my Christian readers:

Chutzpah is from a Yiddish word meaning "intestinal fortitude."

I interrupted my impassioned friend a couple of times for clarification, and, when he brought his case to a close, I answered him.

"Avi, I'll grant you that the New Testament is a bunch of malarkey," I conceded. "I don't really believe it is, but for the sake of this discussion, I'll give you that," I finished my brief opening statement.

"I don't need the New Testament to support my Christian faith. It's you guys who've sent me running after the carpenter from Nazareth. The Hebrew Scriptures and the only Bible the early church had," I reminded him, "are what convinced me Yeshua is the guy!"

For my Christian readers:

Yeshua is the Hebrew rendering of the Greek "Jesus" and is the actual name He was called by while on earth. Of Hebrew origin, the word means "salvation."

And with my volley shot back across his bow, off we went, whacking our religious convictions back and forth in an exhilarating Biblical ping-pong match. We stopped for a breather, frantically opening our cell phones to check the myriad of calls that had tried to disrupt our tournament. Breaking into laughter from disbelief, we both realized that we had been "Torah-tussling" for almost two hours!

We shook hands, gave each other a brotherly hug, walked a few feet toward the parking lot and talked for at least another 15 minutes when Avi offered a proposition: "Let's get together again and do something constructive. Let's talk about doing some music together!"

Now, this was constructive! I laughed, quickly agreeing to his offer and adding that more coffee was definitely in order.

An extraordinary and holy friendship had begun.

Avi and I have so much in common: our love of God, our love of God's people, our love of Torah, the love of our families, and the love of music that is created solely for the adoration of our Creator.

Along with my work as a pastor, I have served as a music director for over half my adult life. My musical background in no way includes any of the incredible and praiseworthy achievements that Avi listed on his resume. My eligibility for being a leader of song within the Christian community is only the qualification noted in the New Testament Greek Scriptures: Luke 7:47. "He who has been forgiven much, loves much." I am humbly overqualified in this manner, and, like Avi, I love worshiping the Lord of Hosts in song.

Avi joined my evangelical Christian band.

I often declare this in front of his Jewish buddies just to goad him and try to get a rise out of his rabbi. My wife and I bought him a shirt reading, **"IT'S OK – I'M WITH THE BAND."** To be more accurate, though, Avi sometimes sings with our music ministry, Wild Branches at 'Night to Honor Israel' celebrations around the country. (Go to

YouTube and type "Wild Branches" in the search setting to see and hear us performing together at the San Diego 'Night to Honor Israel.')

Together we sing the songs of Zion from the Psalms and Hebrew prophets. Though I have been performing some of these songs for over 20 years, they did not sound complete until Avi brought his spiritual portion to the music.

For my Christian readers:

As an aside, take a look here at the book of Revelation 15:3: "They sing the song of Moses, the servant of God, and the song of the Lamb, saying: 'Great and marvelous are Your works, Lord God Almighty! Just and true are Your ways, O King of the ages.'"

As our band finished its first set at one such event, I felt a tap on my shoulder. A handsome, silver-haired gentleman with a large Star of David around his neck leaned towards me and whispered so as to not disturb those around us, "Is the Jewish man singing with your band messianic or a Jew?"

Whenever Avi sings with Wild Branches in front of Jewish audiences, we emphasize in our introductions that Avi is a Conservative Jewish cantor. Even with our explanations, the novelty of seeing and hearing an evangelical Christian band and a Jewish cantor perform together often leaves people a bit puzzled!

I smiled and answered the distinguished inquirer, "He's not a messianic Jew; he is a Jew-Jew!" He quickly made his way back to his wife seated in the middle of the packed auditorium. Out of the corner of my eye, I watched him explain my answer to her. Upon hearing the report, her face lit up with a beaming smile. I read her lips as she exclaimed, "How wonderful!"

I agree. How wonderful, indeed.

Avi and I continue to see each other often. We eat together and drink lots of coffee. I'll grab my 5-year-old grandson, Samuel, and pick up Avi, and his son Ezra, to spend the afternoon doing "man adventures" together with our boys. My wife and I recently helped Avi and his family move all their belongings into a new home they purchased. (You know you are a real friend when you get invited to help someone move!)

Avi and I talk about being married, and we talk about the love and challenges we experience in raising our children. We talk about the sheep in our pastures and how they like to gnaw on their shepherds. We talk about our dreams as men, and we talk about our faith as spiritual brothers. Avi gave me a Torah and together we plunge into the book's Divine streams of revelation.

For my Christian readers:

Judaism refers to the first five books of the Hebrew Bible as the Torah, or the Books of Moses.

Sometimes in formal settings, often over the phone or in casual conversation, we do not miss an opportunity to talk about our faith in the God of Abraham, Isaac, and Jacob. We explore the ways and mysteries of the Almighty, sharing our common and contrasting thoughts.

Avi is no more threatened by my convictions than I am by his. He is a Jew and I am a Christian; and we love, respect, and deeply care for each other.

Some Christians reading this book who already have been speculating that I might be a heretic are now almost certain that I am.

Look: It is like Avi's team is the Arizona Cardinals and my team is the San Francisco 49ers, but we both love football and passionate fellowship about it.

Please keep reading!

Saul, Paul, and Avi

I can guess what some Christians are now thinking, "How can you call yourself an evangelical Christian and not try to convert your poor lost friend Avi? If you really loved him, you would tell him about Jesus!"

Jesus?

Yes, of course, Avi and I have spoken about Jesus, and he knows exactly what I believe about Him. As a matter of fact, he knew what I believed about Jesus before we met and ever discussed the matter.

Rabbis and cantors have an exhaustive education, not only in Hebrew and Aramaic, but many I have met are also conversant with the Greek language. All rabbis are well educated regarding the various aspects of religion and history, and why Jews rejected the Christian Gospels and Christianity in general. Some of them use their knowledge of the Greek language for their study of the Septuagint and their study of the New Testament. I know a number of rabbis who are more familiar with the New Testament than Christians.

For my Christian readers:

The Septuagint is the name given to the Greek translation of the Jewish Scriptures which were translated between 300-200 BC. This translation was produced because many Jews spread throughout the Roman empire were beginning to lose their Hebrew language.

Because "Septuagint" is a Latin word meaning "seventy," the belief is that seventy to seventy-two Jewish scholars were commissioned to carry out the task of translation. The Septuagint was also a source of the Old Testament for early Christians during the first few centuries AD. Many early Christians spoke and read Greek, so they relied on the Septuagint translation for most of their understanding of the Old Testament. The New Testament writers also relied heavily on the Septuagint, as a majority of Old Testament quotes cited in the New Testament are quoted directly from the Septuagint (others are quoted from the Hebrew texts). Some rabbis today study the New Testament in order to give answers to their Jewish congregants concerning our faith in Jesus and why they do not believe Him to be Messiah.

Our Christian faith's "good news" historically has been forced upon the Jews with the edge of a sword, the end of a hanging rope, the hot blaze of a torch, or the calloused toss of a tract.

And I know that Avi has searched the scriptures and does not have the same conclusions as I do regarding *Mashiach*.

For my Christian readers:

Mashiach or Moshiach is Hebrew for the "Messiah," the "Anointed One," the Redeemer of Israel who will appear in history B'Acharit HaYamim, meaning at the "End of Days," to redeem Israel from its enemies and bring peace to all the earth.

And let me clarify this as well: I have not, in my thirty-five years of believing in Christ, yet converted one person. And believe it or not, neither have you. We do not have the power required to grant the personal revelation of Almighty God to another soul. As Christians, we believe this is the exclusive work of our heavenly Father.

Matthew 16:12-17:

> *When Jesus came to the region of Caesarea Philippi, he asked his disciples, "Who do people say the Son of Man is?"*
>
> *They replied, "Some say John the Baptist; others say Elijah; and still others, Jeremiah or one of the prophets."*
>
> *"But what about you?" he asked. "Who do you say I am?"*
>
> *Simon Peter answered, "You are the Christ, the Son of the living God."*
>
> *Jesus replied, "Blessed are you, Simon son of Jonah, for this was not revealed to you by man, but by my Father in heaven."*

As Christians we are commanded:

I Peter 3:15-16:

> *And if someone asks about your Christian hope, always be ready to explain it. But do this in a gentle and respectful way.*

If someone asks.

This scripture in I Peter 3 is my "North Star" for sharing my personal convictions about Jesus with the Jewish people. I pray the instruction becomes your guidance as well. Our words have been historically hollow, dead – and deadly for Jews.

James 2:17:

> "So you see, faith, unless it produces good deeds is dead and useless."

Over coffee one morning, Avi and I were reading through the book of Genesis from the Stone Edition Hebrew Torah translation. If you do not have a Torah, find a Jewish friend and get one. The book is unbelievably rich in color, tone and dialogue. (Many Jews are somewhat familiar with the Hebrew language, so reading their Bible is an enlightening and spiritual banquet for us gentile Christian types.)

Avi was sharing with me wisdom from the Jewish sages, and I was pointing out the portions where Christians see Messianic implications, when Avi shook his head and said,

"Man – you guys see Messiah everywhere!"

I smiled at his comment and answered, "Yeah, we sure do."

"Get over it already!" he laughed.

For my Christian readers:

The Jewish sages are composed of the most prominent rabbis of the 1st century BC through 2nd century AD. Their commentaries concerning the Hebrew Scriptures are written in the Mishna and the Talmud. The Mishna pertains to the Jewish legal code as interpreted from the Scriptures, and the writings of the Talmud explain how to study the Mishna. Jews rely on these writings for all of their understanding of Old Testament theology.

I am a Christian, and Avi is a Jew, and I love him. He is not my project, my rabbit's foot, (those who bless the Jews will be blessed, etc) or my target. He acknowledges the God of Abraham, God of Isaac, and God of Jacob as God alone and as His Heavenly Father. I do as well.

If Avi and I have the same father, then that makes us brothers.

Saul was a Jew in the New Testament who loved Torah yet he hated and persecuted the followers of Yeshua. God had no problem getting Saul's attention; and after He did, Saul became Paul, our beloved apostle.

If my New Testament faith is true, it must also include the faith that only God is able to reveal the things I believe are true to my precious Jewish friend. Exceedingly able to do so considering that, unlike in Saul's case, Avi loves me.

Answering the question:
"What is your real agenda in reaching out to the Jews?"

When asked by the Jewish people, "What is your real agenda in reaching out to the Jews," I sincerely hope more and more Christians will understand why we are being asked this question and will honestly answer, starting with the following portion of the Torah:

Exodus 17:

Now Amalek came and fought with Israel in Rephidim. And Moses said to Joshua, "Choose people for us and go do battle with Amalek. Tomorrow I will stand on the top of the hill with the rod of God in my hand."

So Joshua did as Moses said to him, to do battle with Amalek. And Moses, Aaron, and Hur went up to the top of the hill. It happened that when Moses held up his hand, Israel was stronger; and when he let down his hand, Amalek was stronger. But Moses's hands grew heavy; so they took a stone and put it under him, and he sat on it. And Aaron and Hur supported his hands, one on this side, and one on that side; and he remained with his hands in faithful prayer until sunset. So Joshua defeated Amalek and its people with the

*sword's blade. Moses built an altar and called its name
"HaShem is My Miracle."*

And then we may finish answering their question:

HaShem often uses people to perform His miracles. Christian
Zionists want to be part of the miracle He is doing with the Jewish
people. We want to encourage and join you in the battle against you.
We want to lift your hands; we want to be on this side of you and on
that side of you. Never again will you walk alone. Never again will you
say, 'There is no one for us.' We believe that you are the beloved of
HaShem and the apple of His eye, and we bless you in the name of the
God of Abraham, Isaac, and Jacob.

Question 4

"What can we do about Christians who target us and our children?"

Standard Christian Answer:
The "Jesus talk" begins.

There is no standard Christian answer when asked this question. Christians generally view a question like this one as a golden opportunity to...what else?

Preach.

> *Seventeen Christian preachers visited Israel for the first time in February 2008. One pastor on the trip told a reporter the following: "The ultra-religious Jews take exception to Christianity, literally stating that 'the Nazis took the bodies of Jews but the Christians were trying to steal their souls.' They literally say that," he added in astonishment.*

The statement made by an ultra-Orthodox Jew in Israel left the evangelical pastor from the United States "astonished."

Sadly, he was astonished without reason. This pastor is an extraordinary and wonderful pro-Israel Christian man, but he was astonished because of his upside-down understanding of the comment.

He was astonished because he had no reference point at all, for why would this peace loving, God seeking man within the Jewish faith say such a thing to a peace loving, God seeking man of the Christian faith?

The heartfelt ultra-Orthodox response to the concept of conversion into a faith that has historically done all within its considerable Christian influence to destroy Jews is very rationally stated by their perception that we are attempting to steal the souls of their children.

For my Christian readers:

Religious Judaism, much like Christianity, has numerous denominations within their faith expression: Reform, Conservative, Modern Orthodox, Orthodox, ultra-Orthodox – each of these with varying degrees of theological differences and similarities.

The ultra-Orthodox response is not only a logically reasonable one, it is also nearly impossible for most Jews to think much differently.

My pastor friend might be comforted by the fact that he has much company in his bewilderment.

Many evangelicals don't know where to start in trying to understand the fearful, and rage filled statement of this Jewish father.

We should not be astonished that many Jews feel this way.

We should be astonished and undone that the symbol of our cross has made them feel this way.

The Cross

> So I'll cherish the old rugged cross, till my trophies at last I lay down;
>
> I will cling to the old rugged cross and exchange it some day for a crown

George Bennard, 1873-1958

'The Old Rugged Cross,' was one of the top ten most popular hymns of the twentieth century. For Christians, the cross is the iconic image of God's ultimate act of love.

Christians believe it is the cross of Calvary where Jesus, as the Lamb of God shed His blood and willingly gave up His life for the remission of mankind's sins.

Jews who have any acquaintance with the past two millennia of history also see the cross as a symbol of blood sacrifice. They see it from the experience of the apparently unquenchable Christian thirst for Jewish blood.

They see it from the experience of being **proselytized** by a historic Christian faith that apparently only loves Jews when they are on crosses. Thus, for many Jews, the cross is one of the most horrendous reminders of the 1,900 years of institutionalized Christian abominations that took place under its mandate.

The symbol of the cross has seared itself into the history and DNA of the Jewish people.

Symbols Matter

Symbolic meanings can change, but not by decree. Only by real-time participation in a prolonged and renewed interactive experience with the symbol can the realities of it be changed.

Ask Steve Jobs.

In the late 1960s and 70s, the Apple name and symbol meant only one thing: The Beatles.

Apple Records was a division of the Beatles tax haven of Apple Corp, founded in 1968.

The label released all Beatles records after 1968 and also became the home to many other artists in the years that followed.

In 1977, Steve Jobs chose 'Apple' as the brand name for his new computer company.

And not since the time of Adam, did a man have any idea what he had just bitten into!

Lawsuits with the Beatle's Apple Corp in 1978, 1986-1991, 2001, and the most recent in 2007 have cost Jobs tens of million of dollars.

But it was worth it. Symbols really matter, and symbols really can earn new meanings.

Four long decades after the Beatles shook the world and left their musical and sociological mark in history, now, whenever someone speaks glowingly of "apple," we don't immediately think of the Beatles. We know that person most likely speaks of an inordinantly weird and deeply personal love relationship with all things apple...

"Apple Computer."

The symbol of the old rugged cross solicits as much good will in the experience of the Jewish people as does the Nazi swastika, which for the Jews looks like a Crooked cross.

To change the historic symbolic meaning of the cross as experienced and viewed by the Jewish community will not be as easy as the apple metamorphosis Steve Jobs embarked upon. Changing a symbol of death and horror to one of life and hope will require a fundamental and sustainable change in Christian interaction with Jewish communities. It will first require an innate change within the heart of Christian faith and attitude toward the Jewish people.

I sincerely hope I do not offend my Jewish readers by using the comparison of such a trivial example to attempt to make a point about such a hideous one.

If I have done so, please forgive me.

I only use this story because of its familiarity with my generation and with the hope of challenging prevalent Christian ignorance regarding contemporary Jewish rejection of our Christian Good News' message.The regular e-mails I receive and conversations I have with many pro-Israel Christians who relay their dismay of "the Jew's hatred of Jesus" is alarming and painfully discouraging to me.

I cannot even start to imagine the turmoil a Jew experiences just by the reading of that false assumption in my last sentence.

Jews don't hate Jesus. Jews hate what has happened to them, for so long, from so many people who say they love Jesus.

Conditioned by the Cross

Though conducted in the late 1890s, Dr. Pavlov's research in conditioning and involuntary reflex actions, offers the Christian community insight into the horrendous desecration of the Jewish psyche caused by the Christian history's relentless decimation of their people and faith.

In Dr. Pavlov's famous research, he introduced a neutral object (a bell) and a significant object (dog food!) to a study group (dogs).

He started his experiment by ringing the bell every time he fed the dogs.

Through the repetition of this procedure over an extended period of time, Pavlov discovered that by simply ringing the bell alone (without the presentation of food) the dogs would begin salivating. Pavlov called the dog's reaction to the bell a "conditional response."

Why?

Because they had been organically and psychologically conditioned into believing that every time they heard the ring of a bell the next thing they could expect was food!

The history of the church has conditioned the Jewish people.

I have heard many a Christian quote, "Fool me once, shame on you. Fool me twice, shame on me!"

Consider for a moment our legacy of "fooling" the Jews.

Common sense alone would be much more than sufficient reason for the Jewish community to give serious and long pause before offering the right hand of fellowship to Christians.

The Jewish people are both the writers of the biblical common sense manual, the Book of Proverbs, and the inheritors of an immense God-given intellect.

In addition to the rational trepidation of the Jewish community in regard to the new Christian love for them; the near-uninterrupted regularity with which they have been persecuted by the Christian societies they have lived in has also inflicted them with a self-preserving behavioral response to Christianity.

Due to our appalling failure to "bless the Jewish people," the primary reason our preaching of the cross is repugnant to Jews is not because of what it means to us, but because of what we have made the cross mean to them.

Understanding the Passion

A Jewish friend recently added to my understanding concerning our Passion of the Cross and the Jews, by sharing a very personal story about his mother.

My dear friend, Hal Stein told me:

"One day, many years ago, my sister and our cousin persuaded my late mother to respond to questions they asked about her life in 'the old country.' They taped the session.

"My mother was born in 1902 in what is now known as the nation of Belarus, in a small village about 85 miles south of its capital, Minsk. At that time Belarus (Belorussia back then), bordering Poland, was a province of Russia. The population of my mother's old-world village was made up equally of Christians and Jews, and she grew up with friends of both faiths. One of the childhood experiences she painfully remembered in the taping session related to an experience that took place almost every year on Good Friday.

"As Easter approached, her Christian neighbor down the street would warn my grandmother that there was going to be trouble in the town. She would then pack up their bedding, lock up their house, and she and her three children would move in with the neighbor for the weekend. It wasn't safe for them to stay in their own home.

"Following the Good Friday service, the Christian church-goers, mainly peasants who lived on farms in the outskirts, would stream out of their churches, having just heard a priestly tirade against 'the Jews who crucified Christ.' They would drink vodka and parade through the village...flaming with rage, ransacking and raiding Jewish-owned businesses. Any Jew foolish or unfortunate enough to be on the streets of the village during Good Friday would be attacked and struck down.

"Listening to this particular memory of my mother's

childhood, something became clear to me about certain memories of my own childhood in Sioux Falls, South Dakota.

"I remembered long Sunday drives in the country with my parents. Going through town, whenever we passed a church where people were either entering or exiting, my mother would tense up and look straight ahead, sometimes muttering to herself. No doubt I must have sensed that her tension was related to seeing the churchgoers. We never talked about it, but it probably affected me, as I never wanted to have anything to do with churches, and I declined opportunities to join secular youth groups like Boy Scouts because they met in churches. No words were necessary for her son to understand at a very early age that there was some sort of inherent danger for Jews with churches...and with Christians."

The first realization of my lack of understanding concerning the "passion of the cross" from the Jewish point of view came into focus during the pre-promotion of the film 'The Passion of the Christ.' Like many Christians, I naively believed the uproar about this film from numerous Jewish community leaders was simply due to the fact that a movie about Jesus was coming out in major theaters around the nation.

For crying out loud...most of them hadn't even seen the thing yet and they were complaining about it, I shamefully recall thinking.

I just couldn't feel what the history of The Passion had meant to the Jews.

Excerpt from: MEL'S PASSION

Gibson's making a film on Jesus worries some Jews

By Marvin Hier and Harold Brackman

The passion of Christ — the crucifixion and hours leading up to it — has been used by bigots, including popes and kings, to inflame anti-Semitism through the ages.

A belief that Jews were responsible for crucifying the Son of God led Pope Innocent III to conclude in the early 13th century that Jews should be consigned to a state of "perpetual subservience" as wanderers and fugitives, and made to wear a mark on their clothing identifying them as Jews.

His pronouncement reinforced widespread anti-Semitism that led over the centuries to millions of Jews being burned at the stake and murdered in pogroms throughout Christian Europe.

The Jewish leaders' cries for help sounded like whining to me, and found absolutely no place of compassion or empathy in my heart.

Millions of Jews being burned at the stake and murdered was of course an abhorrent thought to me. But millions of lives cannot be emotionally fathomed, so they often become just a number with six zeros at the end of it unless one of those lives intimately touches yours. And then, one night, that is exactly what happened.

While at a pro-Israel planning meeting, one of our dearest and bravest of friends (a remarkable and remarkably beautiful 70-year-old Jewish woman named Ruth) came into the living room where we were all gathered and quietly sat down. When this particular woman is sitting quietly, we all get worried!

Ruth suddenly burst into tears, and with apologetic sobs asked our forgiveness for her outburst.

"Ruthie," my wife whispered leaning toward our troubled friend.

"What's wrong?"

Ruth tried to speak several times before she could actually continue.

"I am just so worried about this movie that is coming out," she wept.

"Anti-Semitism is growing so quickly and to have another passion play being released around the world at this time is so dangerous to the Jews!" she explained to the room full of confused, dumb *goyim*.

For my Christian readers:

If you are not a Jew, you are a goy. The word goy means "nation" and refers to the fact that goyim are the members of nations, rather than the Children of Israel. Another term for a non-Jew is "gentile."

"And I am so worried about losing the Christian support!" Ruth continued with her fears.

"I'm kind of lost here, Ruth," I candidly confessed.

"Why is the movie frightening to you and what does it have to do with Christian support?" I asked, realizing just how lost I really was.

Ruth then read an article to us that described how Ted Haggard, the President of the National Association of Evangelicals warned Jews that lobbying against the film could cost them evangelical support for Israel.

There is a great deal of pressure on Israel right now, and Christians seem to be a major source of support for Israel... For the Jewish leaders to risk alienating two billion Christians over a movie seems short-sighted.

For anyone to suggest Christian support for the Jewish people is so fickle as to be contingent upon enjoying the same movies as we do, seems "just a little shortsighted" and frighteningly shallow.

We were livid at the bullying remarks coming from the (then) president of the National Association of Evangelicals. And honestly, until that evening, most of us had never heard of Ted Haggard. He heard from all of us by the next day, however, as we each contacted his office with our rage over his dim-witted and mean-spirited remarks concerning Christian support for the Jews.

The room was absolutely silent except for the muffled crying of our dear Ruthie.

And then my wife spoke and asked all of our Jewish friends in the room to forgive us for the sins committed throughout our horrid history with them.

It was the first time in my life I had ever heard a Christian ask Jews for forgiveness.

My wife's words pierced me with their guilty righteousness and I followed in her holy example, asking for their forgiveness as well.

Our gracious Jewish friends quickly attempted to dissuade us from any sense of historic culpability – but it was too late for that.

We had just felt and seen the terrible scarring our history had left upon a real, live Jew for whom we really did care.

The wounds of our friend had wounded our hearts as well, and finally, after twenty years of pro-Israel activism we were beginning to really love the Jews.

Pure, Genuine...and Rare Christian Religion

Some Christian readers are possibly pursing their lips and swaying their heads in condemnation as they smugly consider my psychosomatic enlightenment and ecumenical "love" for the Jews. I can see angry verses flying my way. "But the Bible says this, and the Bible says that about the Jews!"

I'm familiar with the Book.

And I am aware the Bible says many things about many things.

Simply reciting verses in the direction of those we've sinned against is not one of the practices the New Testament encourages or condones. The truth is, Jewish people have never received much genuine religion from our camp.

James 1:26:

If you claim to be religious but don't control your tongue, you are fooling yourself, and your religion is worthless.

James 1:27:

Pure and genuine religion in the sight of God the Father means caring for orphans and widows in their distress and refusing to let the world corrupt you.

The Practice of Target Practice

Especially disconcerting to the Jewish community are Christians who claim love for the Jews yet continue to treat them like nothing more than conversion targets – confirming exactly what many Jews feel they represent to us.

Since the Jews have been the primary recipients of Christian depravity and hatred since the near birth of our faith, you would think Christians could grasp why a *Jesus Tract* slipped under the windshield or shoved into the hand of a Jew is so repugnant to them.

Before confronting a Jew with the enormity of love we claim to have for them, shouldn't every Christian at least say something like, "Hey...sure sorry about hunting down and killing you guys for so long."

In the last few years, there have been numerous well-meaning announcements made from Christian denominations along with (very expensive) full-page ads in major newspapers proclaiming "the Jews' need of salvation." The declarations usually include a full court press for evangelizing Jews with the Gospel message.

These types of publications must swirl the DNA and memories of the Jewish people with grim reminders of being targeted with our Gospel message throughout history.

The notices are usually laced with sentiments of "great love and respect" for the Jews, along with choice New Testament Bible verses. I'm sure they find it frighteningly reminiscent of our previous (and short-lived) Martin Luther Chapter of great love and respect for the Jews.

I'm sure they also wonder how long this current episode of Christian love for them will last – if they don't convert.

For the Jew, history does have a way of repeating itself.

The next time any Christians really feel a need to target a specific group of people, how about a full-page ad like this one:

THE GOSPEL AND THE MUSLIMS

We of the Christian faith want to express our genuine

friendship and love for the peaceful Muslims of the world, but at the same time make known our believe that the threat of militant Islam is a grave danger to the continued existence of the nation of Israel and the entire world.

We now deplore the killing people in the name of God.

We of the Christian faith therefore, now announce that BECAUSE OF OUR LOVE AND PROFOUND RESPECT for the Muslims of the world, we must remind them of our belief in the saving Gospel of Jesus Christ.

We call upon Christians everywhere to help us share our faith with Muslims in this Crusade of Love!

We really, really, really hope and pray that none of the above statements have offended any Muslims, anywhere.

~ This ad is sponsored by a bunch of us who would rather not have our names published. ~

Obviously you will never see Christians run this type of ad. Neither would we run ads that target the sad and lost scientologists of Hollywood. Nor ones that target all the lost workaholic attorneys of New York. Or those that target the lost and out-of-work realtors and mortgage lenders of the nation...

So why *do* we continue to target the Jews and call it loving and respecting the Jews?

Answering the question:
"What can we do about Christians who target us and our children?"

I suggest every Christian take the time necessary to make some close Jewish friends. Real friendships can't happen overnight so you'll really need to be committed to "loving the Jews" if you are going to actually have the experience of loving a Jew. After you have laughed and wept together; attended synagogue and eaten many meals together, worked against anti-Semitism and for the continued security of the nation of Israel together – then ask your Jewish friend if Jews feel loved by us...when they feel targeted by us.

I was once part of a panel discussion at an AIPAC Conference in Washington, DC and during the Q & A, a young, Jewish college student shared the following familiar story:

"Christian groups on our campus often approach us and say they want to work with us," she stated with a sigh.

"The problem is, they are so aggressive with their evangelizing, we all feel as though we are just 'targets' to them," she cautiously continued, wondering if she should be ashamed of her honest confession.

"We appreciate all the help we can get, but what can we say to them to get them to just, you know...help us?" she finished in an almost apologetic tone.

I asked forgiveness on behalf of my Christian faith for the impious chafing this Daughter of Zion had endured on her campus.

I told her the crux of the Christian faith was to make people feel loved by us...not hunted by us.

I paused before answering her question, trying (with little success) to temper my response, "You know what you can do about it?"

"Tell the Christians who can't stop preaching about Jesus – to please stop." I shouted in her defense. (At this point, I thought I heard squeaking from a chair in the direction of another pastor who was also on the stage trying to quietly sneak away from me!)

"Tell those Christians preaching at you that if they really do want to work with you to stop talking and start doing!"

"Remind them that the nation of Israel and the Jewish people are facing very real, grave, and present dangers and you welcome their friendship. Tell them to live exemplary lives as they walk with you, and if you ever have any questions about why they believe as they do you will ask them!"

"Tell them that," I reiterated.

I then finished, "If they really do love you, and really do want to stand with you, they will smile and probably thank you for your honesty. Hopefully they will become trusted friends and demonstrate lives of true Biblical Christian love."

Amen to that hope.

Ephesians 2:10:

For we are God's workmanship, created in Christ Jesus to do good works, which God prepared in advance for us to do.

Question 5

"Why don't you educate the anti-Israel churches?"

Standard Christian Answer:
"I believe everyone has a right to their own opinions, but I don't think there are any churches that are really against Israel." And, believe it or not, the "Jesus talk" begins.

Throwing Kisses and Beating Up Bishops

I received a phone call from a fellow Christian supporter of Israel, inviting me to an evening debate concerning peace in the Middle East. One of Sacramento's most liberal churches was hosting the discussion. The event was open to the general public, and two members of the Jewish community from the college town of Davis would be available to answer questions.

The presentation purported to offer a balanced approach in contrast to a decidedly anti-Israel production the church had previously sponsored. Aware of the reputation and theology of the congregation, we anticipated this follow-up evening would offer anything but an unprejudiced view.

An added incentive for attending the event was the word that our friend Walid Shoebat was in town. This former Palestinian terrorist, now a confirmed pro-Israel Christian, would be joining us at the brawl – uh, church meeting.

For my Christian readers:

As a young man, Walid Shoebat became a member of the Palestinian Liberation Organization. He participated in acts of terror and violence against Israel and was later imprisoned in the Russian Compound, Jerusalem's central prison for incitement and violence against Israel. After his release, he continued his life of violence and rioting in Bethlehem and at the Temple Mount. After entering the U.S., he worked as a counselor for the Arab Student Organization at Loop College in Chicago, continuing his anti-Israel activities.

In 1993, Walid studied the Old Testament as a challenge to convert his wife to Islam. After six months of intense study, Walid realized that everything he had been taught about Jews was a lie. Convinced he was operating on the side of evil, he chose to become an advocate for his former enemy, the Jews.

Go to: www.shoebat.com for more information.

I made some phone invitations to like-minded associates to strengthen our cause. A few hours later, we all met in the Episcopal Church lobby for the event. As we made introductions of Walid and ourselves to the "Very Reverend *someone*," who would be running the show, we noticed the temperature around us drop about thirty degrees and we sensed the evening would bring a head-on clash with our liberal Christian brothers.

The Very Reverend's opening ceremony was not a prayer; rather, he pontificated about Israel's "historic and continued acts of hostility" against the Palestinian people. His solemn vapors filled the room and were quickly fanned into a flame by a man in the front row who identified himself as a Jew.

This man did not mention in his self-introduction that he was also a hater of Israeli Jews, although his feelings were soon made evident. Every hand from our group shot up into the air to answer this self-absorbed Jewish anti-Semite. He was allowed to drone on, uninterrupted in his condemnations pertaining to every aspect of the nation of Israel. The pleased bishop nodded his head in agreement with every profoundly inaccurate accusation made by his front-row advocate as we continued to wave our hands in the air like elementary school children in desperate need of a potty break.

The reverend seemed to find in the audience only those with their hands politely raised. As he called on them, each echoed, not surprisingly, the sentiments of the teacher's pet in the front row.

And so the evening went.

At one point, Walid was finally acknowledged. As he began speaking, his words displayed the authority of the only person in the room who had actually been raised in the Middle East. As he made the argument for Israel's many amazing humanitarian efforts for its Palestinian citizens, Walid was quickly cut off. Another attendee with the 'appropriate' perspective was given permission to talk.

The Jewish guests from Davis were marched to the front of the room like sheep to the slaughter and immediately assaulted with statements rather than questions from an audience that grew more spiteful by the minute. As the couple bravely stood their ground behind a wobbly wooden pulpit set in front of them, the reverend made a comment so grievous that our entire side of the room groaned out loud! As our hands exploded into the air for recognition to speak, he called (*for the third time in a row*) upon his Jew-hating front-row companion – I lost it.

Standing up, I yelled, "**You can't do that!**" as our entire gang of Christian Zionists (plus a couple of Jewish buddies with us) jumped up and started shouting about the injustice of the entire evening. Before we could get kicked out, we slowly walked out of the lecture hall, continuing our rowdy protest.

I threw kisses to the Jewish couple at the front of the hall and cried out, "We love you! We love you! These guys don't represent us – you have many, many Christian friends!"

The two guests from Davis smiled as we marched out the door in our angry parade. They beamed at our passionate outburst, and, I believe, at our professed love for them as well.

For the record: This is not how we usually conduct ourselves, nor is it how we train others to interact with the detractors of Israel...but it sure felt good making such a fuss in that corrupt environment!

We regrouped in the garden area outside the social hall while the dishonest debate continued inside. A few others who apparently agreed with our uprising followed our lead and slowly trickled out of the church social hall. With them came the junior bishop of the cathedral, who had been assigned the 'sacred' task of asking us to leave their property. (I was actually comforted when he referred to the facility as "their" property, seeing that it certainly did not represent a true house of worship!)

I had just finished cooling a heated conversation between a person from our group and a representative from the church who had followed us outside when I heard Walid warn the junior bishop, "Touch me again – go ahead, touch me again and see what happens!"

Frantically zigzagging through the small crowd that was calmly discussing the events of the evening, I grabbed Walid and, wrapping my arms around his considerable shoulders, announced, "Come on, Brother; we're done here."

He tried to shake himself free from my restraint as he continued urging the young bishop to "Touch me one more time." I whispered a Hebrew proverb in his ear, "Do not answer a fool in his folly lest you become like him," and cautioned Walid, "It's already happened, brother; let's get out of here!"

Without waiting for his approval, I pushed and pulled with all of my strength, inching him off the church property. I suddenly felt the resistance in his body slough to the ground as he resigned himself to my unsolicited intervention. Releasing my death grip, we walked together toward the peaceful (and sane) buffer zone of the city-owned sidewalks of Sacramento.

My dear wife, who had been in the thick of the entire episode, was the first one to speak after we silently re-gathered our troops, our thoughts, and our dignity: "There sure is a lot of testosterone here right now!" she laughed out loud.

Yep – there sure was.

The Problem Educating Anti-Semitic Christians

The entirety of the Hebrew proverb that I recited to my friend Walid is as follows:

> Proverbs 26:4-5:
>
> *Answer not a fool according to his folly, lest thou also be like unto him. Answer a fool according to his folly, lest he be wise in his own eyes.*

In other words, there is a time to walk away from those who are expounding foolishness and there is a time to confront them. Hopefully, through our attempts to know the Almighty and recognize His voice, we can be divinely guided through these types of disagreements.

In the story I just shared, none of us were looking all that attentively for guidance from our Maker. That night, however, became a memorial of sorts for our pro-Israel efforts. We did learn a critical truth through the chaos we experienced and the ensuing fireworks that we lit.

We recognized (not for the first time) that there are folks in this world, including Christian folks, who do not reference the same compass as we do. Our north is their south; some things we call righteous, they deem wicked and vice versa. There certainly is opportunity for differences of opinions in our debates, including all topics. There is room for criticizing Israel when she has behaved in a way that is unworthy of her stature as a nation. With that said, however, the pseudo-debates demonizing every action of the nation of Israel do not fall in the category of "difference of opinion." Anti-Semitism in all forms is a dark and wicked sin, damning the soul of man. Clothing the prejudice in political or religious rhetoric neither softens it nor makes the adherence to it any less detestable to the Almighty.

Isaiah 5:20:

Woe unto them that call evil good, and good evil; that change darkness into light, and light into darkness; that change bitter into sweet, and sweet into bitter!

Matthew 6:22-23:

Your eye is a lamp that provides light for your body. When your eye is good, your whole body is filled with light. But when your eye is bad, your whole body is filled with darkness. And if the light you think you have is actually darkness, how deep that darkness is!

Educating the Educable

As Christian Zionists, we have made the decision to invest the best of our time, strength, and efforts in events where we can educate the people most inclined to support the nation of Israel. We refer to this strategy as "reaching the low-hanging fruit." In the Christian community, reaching, teaching, and engaging evangelicals has become our primary target.

Martin Luther employed the word 'evangelical' to identify a specific doctrinal tradition, defining those Christians who left the Roman Catholic Church. Later in his life Luther strayed far from his own convictions regarding the Scriptures' clear and constant heralding of God's everlasting love for the Jewish people.

The word 'evangelical' came from an ancient Greek term for 'good news,' and it meant both the good news of Jesus Christ and the good news regarding the faith of a people who believed they were created to help heal the hurting of mankind. William Wilberforce used the word to describe his faith while fighting British slavery.

For my Christian readers:

I include more of Luther's thoughts concerning the Jews from his diatribe *On the Jews and Their Lies:* "They [rulers] must act like a good physician who, when gangrene has set in proceeds without mercy to cut, saw, and burn flesh, veins, bone, and marrow. Such a procedure must also be followed in this instance. Burn down their synagogues, forbid all that I enumerated earlier, force them to work, and deal harshly with them, as Moses did...If this does not help we must drive them out like mad dogs." – Martin Luther, 1543 (On the Jews and Their Lies)

It is not simply because evangelicals read the Bible that we are passionate supporters of the Jewish people, but it is the way we read it that births a love for Jews within our hearts. The evangelical creed believes in the authority of the Bible as being "God breathed" or inspired by God, and is to be read and understood as such. Because of this core belief, the pro-Israel education of evangelical Christians begins in the study of the Hebrew and Greek scriptures. What an amazing moment when, during the course of such studies, you literally see the lights go on inside the hearts and minds of the congregation! Once an individual has his Biblical paradigm established concerning the Jewish people and the land of Israel, that belief is secured within their personal faith convictions and is near unchangeable.

Evangelicals teach that the Bible is to be interpreted through the same rules followed in everyday conversation.

When the plain sense of Scripture makes common sense, seek no other sense; therefore, take every word at its primary, ordinary, usual, literal meaning, unless the facts of the immediate context, studied in the light of related passages and axiomatic and fundamental truths, indicate clearly otherwise.

These four rules were formulated by Dr. David L. Cooper, the late founder and director of the Biblical Research Society.

For instance, if in the course of a discussion a person tells you a dream he had, you interpret his comments by first understanding he is talking to you about a dream. You comprehend immediately as he relates specifics that he did not actually "eat a two-story tall marshmallow," but this was a scene of his dream. In addition, the dream may appear to have specific meaning – or may be the after-effects of a late-night burrito snack.

Judges 7:13:

And when Gideon was come, behold, there was a man telling a dream unto his fellow, and saying: "Behold, I dreamed a dream, and, lo, a cake of barley bread tumbled into the camp of Midian, and came unto the tent, and smote it that it fell, and turned it upside down, that the tent lay flat."

Evangelicals interpret this portion of Scripture with the understanding that the story is about a dream; i.e., there was not a literal loaf of barley bread that tumbled into a campground and smashed somebody's tent. Neither is this portion of scripture to be taken as a metaphor concerning the trials of life or the dangers of cooking outdoors. It simply is what it is: a dream. This particular dream is then interpreted for us:

Judges 7:14:

And his fellow answered and said: "This is nothing else save the sword of Gideon the son of Joash, a man of Israel: into his hand God hath delivered Midian, and all the host."

We are then told that Gideon, eavesdropping on the entire exchange, takes the dream and interpretation as a sign from Hashem, goes back to his camp, and gets his guys ready to rumble.

Judges 7:15:

And it was so, when Gideon heard the telling of the dream, and the interpretation thereof, that he worshipped; and he returned into the camp of Israel, and said: "Arise;

for HaShem hath delivered into your hand the host of Midian."

In the most basic of guidelines, this process delineates how true evangelicals read the Torah, the Prophets, the Writings, and the Greek scriptures as well.

For my Christian readers:

Judaism refers to the first five books of the Hebrew Bible as the Torah (your Jewish friends will appreciate it if you do not call their scriptures The Old Testament). There are three sections to the Hebrew Bible or, as it is called in Hebrew, the *TaNaKH*: an acronym for Torah, Prophets, and Writings. *Torah* means "teaching" and is God's revealed instructions to the Jewish people. It was given to the children of Israel at Mount Sinai during their exodus from Egypt approximately 3,500 years ago. The Prophets are direct prophecies or recordings of what was said to the prophets, and the Writings are books written by the prophets with the guidance of God.

Evangelical Christians read and understand the parables of Jesus as teaching illustrations. We read and understand the Hebrew books of poetry through the divine prose of parallelisms. The book of Proverbs is a book of observed wisdom and not a book of promises to us. We also know, since the Bible uses anthropomorphic descriptions for the Almighty, such as in Psalm 18 – that God does not have a nose!

Psalm 18:15:

The valleys of the sea were exposed and the foundations of the earth laid bare at your rebuke, O Lord, at the blast of breath from your nostrils.

Christians are supposed to recognize that even in the best of our Biblical conclusions, we see and understand the person of God through a hazy and finite view:

1 Corinthians 13:11-13:

When I was a child, I spoke and thought and reasoned as a child. But when I grew up, I put away childish things. Now we see things imperfectly as in a cloudy mirror, but then we will see everything with perfect clarity. All that I know now is partial and incomplete, but then I will know everything completely, just as God now knows me completely. Three things will last forever – faith, hope, and love – and the greatest of these is love.

How unspeakably tragic that Christianity does not have a legacy of faith, hope, and love toward the Jewish people.

How to Tell Pro-Israel Evangelicals... from the others

Using the same literal interpretation of the Scriptures, evangelicals who read the following verse from Jonah simply believe that God told a great fish to swallow His hesitant prophet and then commanded the fish to hold him captive in its belly for three days and three nights. We might disagree over the type of fish, but we will not argue over the clear narrative describing one very large fish and its swallowing of Jonah.

Some argue, "How could such a thing happen?"

Evangelicals read these things and say, "With God, all things are possible."

Jonah 1:17:

And HaShem appointed a great fish to swallow Jonah, and Jonah was in the stomach of the fish three days and three nights.

So, perhaps needless to say, when we evangelicals muse over the myriad of verses in the Torah that speak of HaShem's everlasting covenants and love for the Jewish people, we simply believe the verses are absolute and indisputable truths.

Genesis 17:7:

I will establish My covenant between Me and you and your descendants after you throughout their generations for an everlasting covenant, to be God to you and to your descendants after you.

1 Kings 10:9:

Blessed be HaShem your God Who delighted in you to set you on the throne of Israel; because HaShem loved Israel forever.

Isaiah 49:14-16:

But Zion said, "HaShem has forsaken me, HaShem has forgotten me."

"Can a mother forget the baby at her breast and have no compassion on the child she has borne?"

"Though she may forget, I will not forget you! See, I have engraved you on the palms of my hands; your walls are ever before me."

We believe the Jewish prophets foretold the worldwide Diaspora of the Jewish people, after which God, one day, would bring them back to the land He had given them:

Jeremiah 16:14-15:

"Therefore, behold, the days are coming," says the Lord, "when it shall no more be said, 'As the Lord lives, Who brought up the children of Israel out of the land of Egypt'; But the days are coming when it will be said...'As the Lord lives, Who brought up the children of Israel from the land of the north and from all the countries to which they have been scattered.' For I will bring them again to their land which I gave to their fathers."

Ezekiel 34:11-13:

For this is what the Sovereign Lord says: "I myself will search for my sheep and look after them. As a shepherd looks after his scattered flock when he is with them, so will I look after my sheep. I will rescue them from all the places where they were scattered on a day of clouds and darkness. I will bring them out from the nations and gather them from the countries, and I will bring them into their own land."

Pro-Israel evangelicals also take to heart the many New Testament verses that remind us of the unique place in the Almighty's heart for His firstborn, the Jewish people:

Romans 9:4-5:

Theirs [the people of Israel] is the adoption as sons; theirs the divine glory, the covenants, the receiving of the law, the temple worship and the promises. Theirs are the patriarchs, and from them is traced the human ancestry of Christ....

Matthew 15:22-28:

(Jesus and the gentile woman)

A Canaanite woman from that vicinity came to him, crying out, "Lord, Son of David, have mercy on me! My daughter is suffering terribly from demon-possession."

Jesus did not answer a word. So his disciples came to him and urged him, "Send her away, for she keeps crying out after us."

He answered, "I was sent only to the lost sheep of Israel."

The woman came and knelt before him. "Lord, help me!" she said.

He replied, "It is not right to take the children's bread and toss it to the dogs."

"Yes, Lord," she said, "but even the dogs eat the crumbs that fall from their masters' table."

Then Jesus answered, "Woman, you have great faith!
Your request is granted." And her daughter was healed from
that very hour.

The dogs, huh?

OK – that's pretty clear.

For evangelicals, it is obvious in the Scriptures that the Jewish
people were and are God's first love; we goyim are plainly His second
choice. Also obvious to us is that HaShem has a continuing relationship
with the Jewish people and a uniquely glorious destiny for them.

Romans 11:1:

I ask then: "Has God rejected his own people, the nation
of Israel? God forbid – may it never be so!"

Romans 11:11:

I say then, "Did they stumble that they might fall? God
forbid – may it never be so!"

Through this form of literal interpretation of the Bible, we establish
our convictions about every aspect of our Christian faith.

Many within the non-evangelical Christian community see the
Bible as inspired by man and riddled with inconsistencies. In so doing,
they tend to embrace a non-literal and broad view of the Scriptures
and thus have a liberal spirituality and worldview. This variety of
theology generally excludes the unique and enormous significance that
evangelicals see placed by the Almighty upon the nation of Israel and
the Jewish people.

The "Other" Evangelicals

A few days after our very successful 2007 Christians United For
Israel, Israel/D.C Summit, President George W. Bush received the
following letter from a group of men identifying themselves as
"evangelical" leaders in the United States.

Letter to President Bush from Evangelical Leaders

President George W. Bush
The White House
1600 Pennsylvania Ave NW
Washington DC 20500

Dear Mr. President:

We write as evangelical Christian leaders in the United States to thank you for your efforts (including the major address on July 16) to reinvigorate the Israeli-Palestinian negotiations to achieve a lasting peace in the region. We affirm your clear call for a two-state solution. We urge that your administration not grow weary in the time it has left in office to utilize the vast influence of America to demonstrate creative, consistent and determined U.S. leadership to create a new future for Israelis and Palestinians. We pray to that end, Mr. President.

We also write to correct a serious misperception among some people including some U.S. policymakers that all American evangelicals are opposed to a two-state solution and creation of a new Palestinian state that includes the vast majority of the West Bank. Nothing could be further from the truth. We, who sign this letter, represent large numbers of evangelicals throughout the U.S. who support justice for both Israelis and Palestinians. We hope this support will embolden you and your administration to proceed confidently and forthrightly in negotiations with both sides in the region.

As evangelical Christians, we embrace the biblical promise to Abraham: "I will bless those who bless you." (Genesis 12:3). And precisely as evangelical Christians committed to the full teaching of the Scriptures, we know that blessing and loving people (including Jews and the present State of Israel) does not mean withholding criticism when it is warranted. Genuine love and genuine blessing means acting in ways that promote the genuine and long-term well being of our neighbors. Perhaps the best way we can bless Israel is to encourage her to remember, as she deals with her neighbor Palestinians, the profound teaching on justice that the Hebrew prophets proclaimed so forcefully as an inestimably precious gift to the whole world.

Historical honesty compels us to recognize that both Israelis and Palestinians have legitimate rights stretching back for millennia to the lands of Israel/Palestine. Both Israelis and Palestinians have committed violence and injustice against each other. The only way to bring the tragic cycle of violence to an end is for Israelis and Palestinians to negotiate a just, lasting agreement that guarantees both sides viable, independent, secure states. To achieve that goal, both sides must give up some of their competing, incompatible claims. Israelis and Palestinians must both accept each other's right to exist. And to achieve that goal, the U.S. must provide robust leadership within the Quartet to reconstitute the Middle East roadmap, whose full implementation would guarantee the security of the State of Israel and the viability of a Palestinian State. We affirm the new role of former Prime Minister Tony Blair and pray that the conference you plan for this fall will be a success.

Mr. President, we renew our prayers and support for your leadership to help bring peace to Jerusalem, and justice and peace for all the people in the Holy Land.

Finally, we would request to meet with you to personally convey our support and discuss other ways in which we may help your administration on this crucial issue.

Sincerely,
Ronald J. Sider, President
Evangelicals for Social Action
(And 29 others – too much space would be taken to list the names here.)

No surprise: On July 29, 2007 the New York Times published the entire letter.

Now that I have reread the letter since its publication, I am again mystified by the intellectual and theological dishonesty of its contents.

Any discussion that includes the phrase "the tragic cycle of violence" concerning the turmoil between the nation of Israel and the Palestinian people or surrounding Arab nations is disqualified from being taken seriously. Period.

(Please see "MESSAGE FROM DAVID BROG," CUFI'S EXECUTIVE DIRECTOR – Page 116)

Next, supporting justice is good. The important question we first need answered is, "Whose concept of justice are we going to use as our standard?"

If I give my daughter a bike for her birthday and someone wants to take it from her, is there justice in allowing the one who wants her bike to take it?

If we are using my standard of justice as a father, and as the giver of the gift, then I say my daughter is justified in her rights to keep her bike. The person who would like to have the bike can disagree with me. He can even try to make a case as to why he needs the bike, but in this case, I am not inclined to adopt his standard of justice should he try and repeatedly take it from her.

Now should my daughter choose to share, or even give the bike to another, that is absolutely her prerogative.

When pro-Israel evangelicals speak of justice concerning the Jewish people and the land of Israel, we start with the conviction that this "bike" was promised to the descendants of Abraham, Isaac, and Jacob.

Genesis 13:14-15:

HASHEM said to Abram, after Lot had separated from him, "Now lift up your eyes and look from the place where you are, northward and southward and eastward and westward; for all the land which you see, I will give it to you and to your descendants forever."

Genesis 15:18-21:

On that day HaShem made a covenant with Abram, saying, "To your descendants I have given this land, From the river of Egypt as far as the great river, the river Euphrates: the Kenite and the Kenizzite and the Kadmonite and the Hittite and the Perizzite and the Rephaim and the Amorite and the Canaanite and the Girgashite and the Jebusite."

Genesis 28:12-14:

And behold, HASHEM stood above it and said, "I am the HaShem, the God of your father Abraham and the God of Isaac; the land on which you lie, I will give it to you and to your descendants."

Exodus 6:8:

And I will bring you to the land I swore with uplifted hand to give to Abraham, to Isaac and to Jacob. I will give it to you as a possession. I am the Lord.

There are many, many verses that reiterate this promise to the descendants of Abraham, Isaac, and Jacob.

Unfortunately, you can call yourself an evangelical and select the verses that are immutable and then select those verses where you perceive God meant something opposite of what He said. And to be honest, many Christians do use selective verse theology to gratify their own philosophical and sociological leanings and to empower the preaching of their own prejudices.

The evangelicals who wrote the above letter to President Bush present an excellent example of religious bias as they claim to embrace the biblical promise to Abraham: "I will bless those who bless you." (Genesis 12:3) Such an odd place they chose to end the quote – right in the middle of the sentence! Is it absentmindedness or convenience that they omit the totality of the promise of Genesis 12:3?

Genesis 12:3:

> I will bless those who bless you **and him who curses you I will curse**.

Their omitted small print of this covenant undeniably changes the profound teaching on justice that the Hebrew prophets proclaimed so forcefully, as well as completely ignores the God-given eternal land grant of Canaan into the hands of the descendants of Abraham, Isaac, and Jacob.

I am intentionally not spending any more time making my argument in suggesting a theological predisposition within the letter my brothers in Christ wrote to the President.

Part of their spiritual definition of "justice" can be attributed to their narrow definition of "oppression." Regarding the land and people of Israel, they simply see Israel as the oppressor and the Palestinian people as *the* oppressed. It is a desire to "free the oppressed" that explains their opinions of and solutions to the Israeli/Palestinian conflict.

Another cause of this type of attitude toward the Jewish people comes from a Christian theological view called Amillennialism.[3] The Amillennialist does not believe in a literal 1,000 year Messianic reign on the earth.

The Biblical views contained within Amillennialism make the notion of Jews having any enduring covenant with the Almighty (apart from faith in Jesus Christ) a sacrilegious thought.

---

[3] I strongly recommend the book *Basic Theology*, by Charles C. Ryrie. It is a wonderful resource for understanding the varying Christian theological views on numerous subjects, including Amillennialism.

Amillennialists believe the yet-unfulfilled Biblical covenants God made with the Children of Israel are either fulfilled spiritually in the church – or that the promises made to the Jewish people need not be fulfilled at all. From the Amillennial point of view, all the promises God made to the Jewish people were conditional covenants, and, because the Jewish people did not meet the conditions required by God for Him to keep His promises, He need not fulfill them.

Pro-Israel Evangelicals differentiate between the conditional covenants God has made with the Jewish people, and the unconditional covenants He has made with them.

The conditional covenants of God are understood through the prescribed agreement of "If you do such and such – then I will do so and so."

An unconditional covenant is defined as a unilateral covenant, "I will do such and such!"

It is a promise, or series of promises that God has made with the Jewish people whereby He unconditionally obligates Himself to bring to pass definite promises made to His covenanted people. These promises are guaranteed to be fulfilled based exclusively upon the intentions and integrity of The One making the promise.

Answering Fools in Their Folly

Proverbs 26:5:

Answer a fool according to his folly, lest he be wise in his own eyes.

There are times we Christian Zionists must weigh in on matters of anti-Israel rhetoric and activities within the Christian community. There are times we must "answer fools according to their folly."

In response to the letter I just referenced, David Brog, immediately sent out the following e-mail to our thousands of supporters, including many national Christian leaders who then forwarded it to hundreds of thousands within their flocks.

MESSAGE FROM DAVID BROG, CUFI'S EXECUTIVE DIRECTOR

Last Friday, a group of over thirty evangelical Christians wrote a letter to President Bush to "correct a serious misperception among some people ... that all American evangelicals are opposed to a two-state solution and the creation of a new Palestinian state." They made reference to the "cycle of violence" in the region and the fact that "Israelis and Palestinians must both accept each other's right to exist."

It's no coincidence that this letter was sent barely a week after our second annual Washington, DC, summit. As we grow, those who disagree with us, however few they may be, will be shouting at the top of their lungs in an effort to equal the sound of 4,500 Christians gathered in the DC Convention Center cheering our cause. They will not succeed.

This letter raises many questions. But the biggest question is this – where have these people been for the past decade? Don't they realize that Israel not only accepted the Palestinian right to exist, but repeatedly sought to give the Palestinians land on which to build their state? At meetings in Camp David in 2000, Prime Minister Ehud Barak offered the Palestinians 100% of Gaza, over 90% of the West Bank, and sufficient land from Israel's Negev Desert to compensate for every inch of the West Bank that would not be returned. He also offered them control of the Muslim areas of Jerusalem. What was the Palestinian response to this unprecedented offer? Celebration? A counter-offer? No – sadly, the Palestinians chose this juncture to start the second intifada with a spree of bus bombings and killings.

In 2005, Israel actually did pull out of the Gaza Strip and left it to Palestinian rule. What did the Palestinians do? Did they take over the Israeli greenhouses left behind and begin to build their economy? Did they take this opportunity to demonstrate that they wanted to live side-by-side with

Israel? No – sadly, Hamas terrorists took over the Gaza Strip and now use it as a base from which to launch rocket attacks against Israel.

The letter's use of the term "cycle of violence" is particularly troubling. There is a fundamental difference between terrorists on the one hand and Israeli and American soldiers on the other. The goal of terrorists is to kill as many civilians as possible, and when they succeed in doing so they celebrate. Israeli and American soldiers seek to stop the terrorists from killing innocent civilians. When our soldiers kill civilians, however few, it is a tragic error. As both of our nations continue to fight terrorists around the world, we must never permit the morally callous equation of these opposite roles.

We all want peace. No one wants peace more than the Israelis who live on the front lines. But wishes don't always come true. To survive in this world, love is important. So is understanding. And so is realism. Sadly, given this track record, only a dreamer or a foe would press Israel for further concession at this juncture. I pray that those who signed this letter are the former."

Pastor John Hagee immediately drafted and is circulating a letter to President Bush, which will demonstrate the widespread support for CUFI's position that America not pressure Israel for further concessions at this time.

Beyond this, our best response is to continue our work. Let us continue to build and to grow. Let us demonstrate with results that we have the momentum and that we represent the future.

Thank you, David Brog. There is a time to answer fools in their folly.

CUFI Sends a Letter to the President

Pastor John Hagee penned a letter to President Bush and had a courier deliver it to his office. The CUFI document was signed by all our Christian United For Israel State and Regional Directors (whose names are also too numerous to list.)

July 26, 2007

President George W. Bush
The White House
1600 Pennsylvania Avenue NW
Washington, DC 20500

Dear Mr. President,

I want to thank you for your gracious greeting of the Christians United for Israel Washington Israel Summit conducted in Washington D.C. last week.

Some 4500 delegates from every state in the union came to Washington for the purpose of meeting our senators and congressmen to express our support for the State of Israel and the Jewish people of the world.

Mr. President, we the undersigned specifically write this letter to state we are opposed to America pressuring Israel to give up more land to anyone for any reason.

What has the policy of appeasement ever produced for Israel that was beneficial? In the League of Nations Mandate for Palestine, Israel was given a parcel of land for a new state. The Arabs protested so loudly 4/5ths of that land was given to create what is now Jordan.

Did it bring good will to Israel? No! The day after Israel was declared a state it was attacked by five Arab armies in an attempt to murder the Zionist dream in the birth canal.

When Israel left Lebanon it did not produce peace. It has strengthened Hezbollah on its northern border, a terrorist army sworn to the destruction of Israel and the death of all Jews.

When Israel left Gaza it strengthened another terrorist army, Hamas, trained and funded by Iran whose covenant calls for the destruction of Israel.

Simply stated, land for peace is a failed policy of the past that has produced nothing but more war.

Under the current circumstances, we feel a two state solution would be unwise. Hamas rules the Gaza Strip and Hezbollah has been rearmed by Iran and is preparing for war at this moment. Mahmoud Abbas and his Fatah movement have until very recently actively participated in suicide attacks against Israeli civilians through the Al Aqsa Martyr's Brigade.

The prerequisite for peace with Israel should be:
1. To recognize Israel's right to exist.
2. To cease and desist from all acts of terrorism.
3. To be willing to be governed by the rule of law from the community of nations.

We recognize the crisis in the Middle East has been and will be one of the great political dilemmas of our time. We pray for you Mr. President that God will give you the wisdom of Solomon for this crisis and that a just and lasting peace will come in our time for Israel.

Most Sincerely,

Dr. John C. Hagee
National Chairman
Christians United for Israel

CHRISTIANS UNITED FOR ISRAEL • P.O. BOX 1307 • SAN ANTONIO, TX 78295
PHONE 210-477-4714 • FAX 210-477-4713 • EMAIL INFO@CUFI.ORG • WWW.CUFI.ORG

There is Also Hope among Non-Evangelicals!

In CUFI's mandate to gather support for Israel from the Christian communities across our nation, we continue to see wonderful stories of hope spring up from some of the most unexpected sources.

Christians United For Israel is working to set up programs on college campuses all across the nation. One of our first CUFI on-campus initiatives was birthed at the impressive University of Texas-Austin. The student-staffed CUFI Executive Board of Directors is made up of practicing Jews and Christians, and 95 percent of them are Democrats. An additional and wonderful surprise to us is that almost all our Christian leaders involved on this particular campus were from non-evangelical churches! These are young men and women who have realized the Biblical mandate to love and support the Jewish people outside their denominational affiliation and theology.

This gold-mine discovery is so recent that we have not yet fully developed a strategy to reproduce the model, but just knowing there are pockets of support outside the mainline carriers of our message has invigorated our resolve to gather and train all of the pro-Israel Christians forces within the United States. At the 2008 Christians United For Israel DC Summit there were over 250 students in attendance representing more than 130 colleges from across our nation who are standing with Israel.

Answering the question:
"Why don't you educate the anti-Israel churches?"

Here is our painful and true answer: The antidote for the anti-Israel churches within our Christian community is not simply education. We wish it were that straightforward. The anti-Israel attitudes within Christianity are often due to theological persuasions, which produce and feed anti-Israel and anti-Semitic prejudices. We will not abandon the necessity to confront the Christian detractors of Israel, nor have we given up on winning them over from their poorly lit inclinations. Please realize, the difficulty in doing so has more to do with matters of the heart than with education.

We believe our first and most important commission involves the 50 million Evangelicals in the United States whom we will continue to gather, educate, and then train so they can become political advocates for the nation of Israel and the Jewish people

Question 6

"How are Christian Zionists trying to influence Israeli politics?"

Standard Christian Answer:
This question will usually get you a very long religious discourse on why the nation of Israel must not give up a single inch of land in the attempts to negotiate peace with its Arab neighbors.

Christians United For Israel

Christians United For Israel (CUFI) has been called "one of the most politically influential Christian grass-roots organizations in America." (Bill Moyers Journal – Christians United for Israel (CUFI) PBS March 7, 2008)

CUFI is a single-issue pro-Israel coalition made up of many diverse and autonomous Christian ministries. One of the main goals of CUFI is to turn praying pro-Israel evangelicals into politically active pro-Israel evangelicals.

CUFI's public policy efforts include:

CUFI's annual Washington-Israel Summit in Washington, D.C., that enables CUFI members to speak personally with their elected officials about their concerns for Israel's security and to express their support of Israel's right to the land by Biblical Mandate.

CUFI's Rapid Response Alerts that mobilize CUFI members at critical junctures throughout the year to generate millions of phone calls and e-mails requesting support for Israel from the Administration and Congress.

CUFI's State government efforts. Even state governments can play a role in protecting America and Israel, especially by divesting their public funds from companies that do business with Iran. CUFI will mobilize our members to speak with their state leaders about the need to engage in terror-free investing

Christian Political Responsibility

Influencing the political policies of the United States government is both an obligation and responsibility of a U.S. citizen.

For Christians, there is also Biblical precedence for participation:

- Moses prayed and petitioned the Pharaoh...to free the Children of Israel.

- Esther prayed and petitioned the king...and saved the Jewish people.

- Nehemiah prayed and petitioned the king...for the rebuilding of Jerusalem.

- John the Baptist prayed and petitioned the king...concerning unrighteousness in his role as a leader over the Jewish people.

In like manner, the members of CUFI are exhorted to pray and petition our local and national leaders in matters of concern to the nation of Israel.

It is disingenuous and disobedient for a Christian to say he believes in "blessing the Jews" and yet does nothing to support those words.

James 2:17:

"...faith by itself, if it is not accompanied by action, is dead."

Matthew 25: 35-36:

"For I was hungry and you gave me something to eat, I was thirsty and you gave me something to drink, I was a stranger and you invited me in, I needed clothes and you clothed me, I was sick and you looked after me, I was in prison and you came to visit me."

Sadly, there are many Christians who view any type of political involvement or activism as a waste of spiritual time. The seeds of this apathy and lack of love for our nation have come to fruition as we now witness the disintegration of our national morals that is leading to the frightening collapse of principled reasoning within our society.

Hidden Christian Political Strategies

Members of the Jewish community often contemplate the possibility of hidden long-term political strategies Christian Zionists may have, including the infiltration of Israeli politics.

My initial introduction to CUFI founder, Pastor John Hagee and the immediate aftermath will clarify this legitimate concern. Though I knew very little about Pastor Hagee, what I did know left me deeply impressed. I had some knowledge of him from watching his television ministry and having read about an organization he was starting called Christians United For Israel (CUFI). I was especially intrigued as I read about his vision for CUFI to become the "Christian AIPAC."

For my Christian readers:

For more than half a century, the American Israel Public Affairs Committee, (AIPAC) has worked to help make Israel more secure by ensuring that American support remains strong. From a small pro-Israel public affairs boutique in the 1950s, AIPAC has grown into a 100,000-member national grassroots movement described by *The New York Times* as "the most important organization affecting America's relationship with Israel." (www.aipac.com)

Bashert

For my Christian readers:

Bashert – Yiddish word that means destiny.

After participating in a panel discussion at the Washington, D.C., Convention Center, my wife and I were whisked through a maze of cavernous hallways and suddenly came upon Pastor Hagee finishing up a conversation he was having with an orbit of people circled around him.

We were quickly introduced and almost immediately I experienced the calm pull of Pastor Hagee's presence. After just a few minutes of conversation, he made the following announcement:

"Brother Victor," he entreated me with his rich and sincere Texas-grandpa tenderness.

"I believe the Lord has sent you to be my California Director for Christians United For Israel," he beamed.

Caught completely off guard I stammered, "Pastor Hagee, it is such an honor to meet you, but I can't be your California Director."

To tell the truth, at that exact time in my life my wife and I had just been tossed under the "church bus" by a group of Christian leaders and "friends" we had served with for over twenty years. We were not looking to direct anything and were only ministering in DC under official protest to the Almighty. Bruised, battered, and bewildered, I had made it very clear to our Maker that I was not going to pastor any longer. My dear wife had officially and permanently retired from her position as a "pastor's wife."

Apparently, God had not yet read our prayer memo.

"Well, that's alright," Pastor John answered gently, leaving me feeling as if I had just accepted his unbelievably flattering proposal.

"It's a big state so how 'bout we just cut it in half and make you the Northern California Director for Christians United for Israel?" he pressed onward, grinning at me like I was going to say "yes."

"Pastor Hagee, you are breaking my heart here, but there is just no way I can..." I was interrupted before I could finish.

"No...no, I understand perfectly, Pastor," Pastor Hagee graciously kept me from feeling worse about myself than I already was feeling.

"We are all busy men," he acknowledged.

Right.

I've traveled with Brother Hagee, and his "busy" and my "busy" are not even part of the same solar system!

"What do you think about being our Sacramento City Director for Christians United For Israel?" he persisted – inching a bit closer to me and smiling like a big, friendly bear.

Recognizing that I was standing before a force considerably more formidable than myself, I sort of lied and answered, "Well, that is something I might be interested in doing."

"Let me pray about it with my wife and some of my friends back home in Sacramento, and I'll let you know," I think I lied again.

At this time of my life, I was really unsure about...well, just about everything. But I was pretty sure this was going to be the last time I would ever see Pastor John Hagee.

ONE WEEK LATER:

I received the following letter from CUFI just a few days after returning home from Washington, D.C.:

> *Dear Pastor Victor,*
>
> *It was wonderful meeting you and your beautiful wife, Marita, in Washington, D.C.*
>
> *We so look forward to working with you as our* **Christians United For Israel California Director,** *and ask that you contact us as soon as possible to let us know where you are at with our proposal.*

I laughed.

I laughed and then considered the fact that we had not prayed about the request from Pastor Hagee. We really had not even thought about it, but recognized that we needed to do both. So, as my wife and I began to consider the opportunity before us, one day, to my shock, she announced "she was all in." We included our best friends in the fellowship of our decision-making and they too felt I should accept the position. I gathered all the information I could about the one-month-old ministry of CUFI and came up with only one question that needed answering to finalize my decision.

The Matter of National Sovereignty

The notion of CUFI becoming a "Christian AIPAC" exhilarated me. Having attended AIPAC conferences for many years and seeing the unparalleled success they had in educating our nation's leaders regarding the nation of Israel, I believed CUFI was being born with heaven's assistance to begin something wonderful and profound between Christians and Jews.

As strongly as I believe in my Christian responsibility to participate in the policy making of the nation of my citizenship, I had great hesitation in becoming a part of CUFI, not knowing the organization's stance on influencing Israeli national policy. I called the CUFI office and spoke with one of its national leaders, Steve Sorenson.[4]

Without wasting any time, I inquired, "Steve, what is CUFI's position on the pro-Israel Christian movement attempting to influence Israeli political policy?"

"Well, Pastor Victor, there's this little matter of national sovereignty that Pastor Hagee and all of us here have great respect for," he began.

"Those are not our children going to war and risking their lives for that nation, and I do not believe we have any right to tell the democratically elected Israeli government how to run their country," Steve finished, passionately presenting the official CUFI philosophy on Christian Zionist meddling with Israeli politics.

---

[4] Sorenson served in the United States Air Force Intelligence Community for over twenty-two years with the Electronic Security Command. He finished his distinguished career as the command's senior Electronic Signals expert, establishing training and evaluation standards for his Air Force specialty. Steve has worked for the last twenty-five years with Pastor Hagee and serves as the Administrative Director for the Cornerstone Church leadership ministry with almost 400 groups and 5,000 people under his direction. Sorenson is also one of Christians United For Israel's national leaders.

"What CUFI will be doing, however, is petitioning the leaders of our nation to neither entice nor coerce the government of Israel into doing anything they do not feel is in Israel's best interest," he stated with conviction.

"Brother, that is really good to hear," I answered, realizing that I had just become the CUFI California Director.

Christian Theology and the Land of Israel

In the never-ending "land for peace" negotiations between Israel and Arab leaders, the thought of Israel changing its borders is attacked with a religious zeal from most pro-Israel Christians and many Jews. The emotional froth this topic induces is due to a Biblical theology concerning the God-given inheritance of Eretz Israel to the Jewish people.

For my Christian readers:

Eretz Israel – (Hebrew) "Land of Israel." When Christians speak of "Israel" they may be referring to Jews, the nation of Israel, or the physical land of Israel. When Jews speak of Israel, the land...they refer to it as "Eretz Israel."

The theology of God gifting the land of Israel to the Jewish people is anchored in Genesis and confirmed throughout the Hebrew Scriptures.

Genesis 12:7:

...HaShem appeared to Abram and said, "To your offspring I will give this land."

Genesis 13:14-15:

"...And HaShem said unto Abram, after that Lot was separated from him: 'Lift up now thine eyes, and look from the place where thou art, northward and southward and

eastward and westward; for all the land which thou seest, to thee will I give it, and to thy seed for ever.'"

Genesis 17:7-8:

"And I will establish My covenant between Me and thee and thy seed after thee throughout their generations for an everlasting covenant, to be God unto thee and to thy seed after thee. And I will give unto thee, and to thy seed after thee, the land of thy sojournings, all the land of Canaan, for an everlasting possession; and I will be their God."

Jeremiah 15:15:

"As HaShem liveth, that brought up the children of Israel from the land of the north, and from all the countries whither He had driven them'; and I will bring them back into their land that I gave unto their fathers."

Lecturing the Jews

The simplified version of this land issue espoused by many pro-Israel Christians (and religious Jews) goes like this:

1. God gave the land of Canaan (Israel) to the Jews.
2. Therefore, they must not give away an inch of it to anyone, for anything.

This sound-bite theology often encourages Christian supporters of Israel to belittle the Israeli government in their willingness to consider giving up land in their righteous hunger for peace. The bombastic pretension that we Christians have more political wisdom or a deeper concern for the welfare of the Israeli people than the Israeli people themselves is deeply distressing.

From The American Thinker 2008
By **James Lewis** July 29, 2005

The day before yesterday, we are told, the Church of the Disciples of Christ demanded that Israel tear down its security fence, which has saved countless of Jewish women and children from being blown to smithereens. Twisting the words of Ronald Reagan, Minister William McDermet III of Panama, N.Y., shouted into the microphone to the assembled delegates,

"Say to Ariel Sharon, 'Tear down this wall!!'"

Well, the Rev. McDermet is either a fool or a demagogue, but I suspect the latter, since even a fool can distinguish between a defensive wall and a prison wall. It is difficult to imagine the towering heights of spiritual arrogance required for an American minister, living fat, dumb and happy 6,000 miles away from any danger, to demand that the people of Israel expose the lives of their children to endless terrorist assaults. © *American Thinker 2008*

A Sense of How It Feels

On September 7th, 2007, Osama bin Laden released another one of his bizarre YouTube lectures to the world. In the video, he appeals to the citizens of the United States to convert to Islam.

I invite you to embrace Islam. It will also achieve your desire to stop the war as a consequence, because as soon as the warmongering owners of the major corporations realize that you have lost confidence in your democratic system and have begun to look for an alternative, and this alternative is Islam, they will run after you to please you and achieve what you want...to steer you away from Islam.

Osama bin Laden

Christians (and others) were shocked with his self-righteous and preposterous proposition.

Consider your emotions upon hearing bin Laden's assumed superiority in his Islamic altar call. Why would anyone entertain leaving their faith to join bin Laden's political interpretation of Islam that expresses its tenets with the spilling of so much blood?

What can he possibly believe we would find compelling about his expression of faith?

Now consider your emotions in light of our barbaric Christian history with the Jews and you have possibly experienced, in the minutest of ways, how it feels for Jews to be lectured by Christians.

It is my fervent prayer that we pro-Israel Christians practice comprehending the astonishing longsuffering the Jewish people have endured with us.

I also hope, that, before we tell Israelis what they should do with the land of Israel, we might study the complexities of the limited options the leaders of Israel face while attempting to secure peace for their nation. It is both naïve and arrogant for U.S. citizens to tell the democratic nation of Israel how it should govern the nation or use the land God has given them.

Standing with Israel

On a recent trip to the Holy Land, my wife and I found ourselves in a small group of national Christian leaders invited by Pastor Hagee to meet with Prime Minister Ehud Olmert.

Our passports had to be examined by the Israeli government three weeks before we were to visit with the Prime Minister, and the on-site search they put us through when we actually arrived at the Knesset building was extensive, to say the least.

Two of the Prime Minister's brilliant young staffers engaged us as we entered the official conference room. While trying to answer all our non-stop questions, they also informed us of the current events of the day.

Constantly glancing at their watches, they announced with deferential smiles, "As soon as the Prime Minister steps into the room, we will immediately stop speaking."

Moments later, Prime Minster Olmert entered, and he and Pastor Hagee warmly greeted each other as old friends do.

(I am not prone to going all goo-goo while in the presence of politicians or people of fame, but my spirit was definitely registering this moment as an important one.)

Pastor Hagee and the Prime Minister have a long history, and they spoke freely and respectfully with each other. The Prime Minster looked very weary, but his face turned tranquil as Pastor Hagee rehearsed with passion the recent accomplishments of Christian Zionist support for the nation of Israel.

Toward the end of our meeting, Pastor Hagee smiled and said, "Mr. Prime Minister,we want you to know that the State Department of our government does not always speak for us. If, in the talks with your neighbors, you should ever decide that it is not in Israel's best interests to give up any more land in the hopes of peace – we will support your decision. We represent mainstream America and it can never get too hot for us when standing with you!"

Prime Minister Olmert leaned back in his plush Prime Minster's chair, grinned from ear to ear, and near laughing answered, "Pastor Hagee, you evangelical Christians are the best friends Israel has!!"

In the Book of Genesis, Aaron and Hur lifted the hands of Moses as he wearied during the battle with Amalek.

We had just lifted the hands and heart of Prime Minister Olmert.

God's Judgment on Dividing the Land of Israel

There is sound Biblical teaching concerning the fulfillment of God's promise to Abraham and his descendants inheriting the land.

There is also sound Biblical teaching that warns of God's judgment upon those who divide the land of their inheritance.

> *In those days and at that time, when I restore the fortunes of Judah and Jerusalem, I will gather the gentiles (nations) and bring them down to the Valley of Jehoshaphat. There I will enter into judgment against them concerning my inheritance, my people Israel, for they scattered my people among the nations and divided up my land.*
>
> Joel 3:1-2

Take note: It is "all nations," the gentiles, who will be gathered and judged for dividing up the land.

The land has been given to the Jews to populate, govern, and do with, as they will.

There is no prohibition warning the Jews of "giving up the land."

The boundaries of Israel expanded and contracted during the reign of King David and he was never chastened by the Almighty for allowing the boundary changes.

It is critical for Christian Zionists to petition the United States government to respect Israel's sovereignty in making their own decisions regarding the security of their nation – including the keeping or giving up of land.

But the Land Belongs to the Jews!

As a Christian Zionist, the land was always an extremely simple issue for me.

Over twenty-five years now, it held a theologically secure, safe, and uncomplicated place in my heart.

The land belongs to the Jews. Period.

For many Christians, this is a very simple, safe, and uncomplicated issue:

- Simple for us because it cost us nothing to believe it;

- Safe for us because we don't live there and giving or keeping the land does not involve the blood of our family or friends;

- Uncomplicated for us because our lives have never been personally touched by our theology about the land.

Holding on to simple thoughts is not necessarily a problem. Demanding others to live by our thoughts...now that's a problem.

Proverbs 19:2:

It is not good to have zeal without knowledge, nor to be hasty and miss the way.

In the zeal of the Christian pro-Israel movement to love the Jewish people, I have observed how we often run out of the gate without knowledge. And as warned in the Scriptures, in our zeal, I fear we sometimes miss the way.

Gaining Knowledge

I received an invitation to spend the day with Dr. Yossi Olmert – brother of Israeli Prime Minister Ehud Olmert. I flew to Los Angeles and found myself sitting around a table with about fifteen other pastors and Jewish leaders; listening, learning, and gaining knowledge from Dr. Olmert.[5]

With pained resolve from firsthand experience, Dr. Olmert spoke of the horrors of terrorism and the necessary steps to prevent the ongoing slaughter of his Jewish brethren. He spoke of "the security barrier" and its astonishing effect of reducing successful terrorist attacks.

He told of the 8,000 brave Israeli Jewish citizens who had been living in Gaza and the 15,000 Israeli Defense Force soldiers required to be stationed there daily for their protection. He reminded us of the over one million Palestinians who lived on the same stretch of land...and the painful decision to remove the Israeli communities from the area.

"It just didn't make sense anymore," he whispered.

"It had depleted our resources and our morale," he almost wept.

"And the nation of Israel has not been born to rule over other people," he soundly reminded us.

"The recent consolidation of Israeli citizens out of Gaza was a matter of land for life," Dr. Olmert admitted.

---

[5] Dr.Yossi Olmert is a well-known expert on the modern Middle East, Islamic militants, terrorism, the Palestinian issue, and US-Israel relations. He received his Ph.D. from the prestigious London School of Economics and graduated from the Hebrew University Magna Cum Laude. Dr. Olmert taught in many well-known universities both in Israel and abroad, including Tel Aviv University, The Hebrew University, Cornell University, City College New York and York University in Toronto. Dr. Olmert held several senior positions in the Israeli government including Director of Communications for Prime Minister Shamir and Policy Advisor to Defense Minister Arens.

There was no expectation of real peace from this new equation but rather the simple realization: the security barrier saves Israeli lives and stops terrorist attacks. Since construction of the anti-terrorist fence commenced, there has been over a ninety percent reduction in successful terrorist attacks where construction has been completed.

"The number of Israeli and Palestinian deaths has dramatically dropped – along with the crime of car thefts," he mentioned as an unexpected statistic.

Our hearts were deeply touched with his passion and pain. While sitting at this table, I began to feel "knowledge being added to my zeal" concerning Eretz, Israel. Because of Dr. Yossi, my simplistic, impersonal "land" theology was becoming personal.

The Land God Has Given Us

God has given each of us a land.

It is a land with specific borders, a gift to each of us, and we will one day give an account for our stewardship over it – as will the citizens of Israel for the land they have been given.

Upon the land God has given me rests a wonderful 101-year-old house. We love our home, although it rests in a tough, high-crime, inner-city neighborhood amongst a very diverse population, in an area where we have lived for over twenty years.

Our neighborhood is not known as a "peaceful" region. We are better known for our gangs and prostitutes, guns and poverty. We do our best, however, to live in peace with all our neighbors, and as Christians we daily try to find ways to show them the love of Jesus.

Our house is right in the middle of a large Pakistani Sunni Muslim community.

Not our plan. God is funny like this with us.

Their Sunni Muslim faith is built upon The Five Pillars of Islam.

- Shahadah: is the Sunni Muslim "profession of belief" which is recited daily. "There is no God except for Allah, and Muhammad is the messenger of Allah."

- Salah: is the Muslim requirement to pray five times a day at fixed times: dawn, noon, mid-afternoon, sunset, and nightfall.

- Zakah: consists of spending a fixed portion of one's wealth for the benefit of the poor or needy.

- Sawm: three types of ritual and ascetic fasting.

- Hajj: a pilgrimage to the al-Masjid al-Haram mosque in Mecca, Saudi Arabia at least once in a lifetime for those who can afford to do so. Muslims believe Abram was commanded by Allah to offer up Ishmael at this location.

My neighbors pray five times a day facing Mecca. I am moved to pray for them each time I hear their cars honking to gather at the mosque. I have seen them numerous times with their prayer carpets spread in a public setting, should they be unable to gather together during their commanded times of worship.

They pay cash for all their purchases (per Islamic law), including the many properties they own in our neighborhood.

Their children are required to memorize the entire Quran by their early teens. The Quran is written in Arabic; their children only speak Urdu and English. They memorize the 5,000+ verses within the Quran phonetically.

Some of their women wear burqas (head-to-foot outer covering garments) and all of them cover their heads with shawls whenever they come outside.

If you were to close your eyes and walk down our street, oftentimes the tantalizing smells of curry and sounds of Arabic music might cause you to imagine you had been transported into a Middle Eastern village.

They respect our family deeply, and because they have observed our faith as sincere and authentic, they believe we will convert to the Muslim faith when "Jesus returns to rule over the earth."

Yep, when Jesus returns.

It is a part of Muslim end of days messianic theology. (See Question #8)

In their eschatological (end of days) view, however, Jesus is Muslim.

From the Quran: "Behold! The angels said, 'Oh Mary! God gives you glad tidings of a Word from Him. His name will be Christ Jesus, the son of Mary, held in honor in this world and the Hereafter, and in (the company of) those nearest to God. He shall speak to the people in childhood and in maturity. He shall be (in the company) of the righteous... And God will teach him the Book and Wisdom, the Law and the Gospel" (Quran 3:45-48).

She said, 'My Lord! How can I have a son when no man has ever touched me?' He said, 'It will be so. God creates whatever He wills. When He decides on something, He just says to it, "Be!" and it is.'" (Aal `Imran 3:47)

Christ Jesus the son of Mary was (no more than) an Apostle of Allah and His Word which He bestowed on Mary and a Spirit proceeding from Him: so believe in Allah and His Apostles. (Quran 4:171)

As a Christian, I clearly believe differently from these wonderful, devout neighbors of mine. I love them and pray for them...often with tears. They speak and exhibit their love for me as well.

But what if...?

- But what if rather than being peace-loving Muslims, these neighbors of mine were militant Muslims and had a history of attacking my family and home?
- But what if the lives of my family members were at constant risk of being killed by these attacks?
- But what if I realized that I could no longer protect my family within the boundaries of my home, but I believed that I could protect them if we moved into the teen center, just behind the high wall of our backyard?

One day I began contemplating this comparison of my home and family with everyday life in Israel and the daily decisions their leaders confront in protecting Israeli citizens.

I posed this make-believe scenario to an unsuspecting Christian brother who was in a park, participating in an "anti-Olmert, pro-Israel" rally (an example of a self-righteous Christian oxymoron from my point of view.)

"How long would you think about moving your family out of your house and behind a backyard fence if you thought it would save your family's lives in this circumstance?" I inquired of him.

"Well," he scratched his chin, wrinkled his forehead, and squinted his eyes in thought.

"I'm not sure," he answered, either lying or forgetting to turn his brain on.

"You've got to be kidding me!" I exclaimed incredulously.

"If you truly believed your family would be safe behind a fence, you wouldn't think about it for a moment. You would run with them out of the house God gave you! You'd do it because the life of your family is a higher priority before the Almighty than the sticks and stones and dirt of the home He gave you and you know it," I moralized.

Israel's Attempts to Secure Peace

A quick review of the concessions Israel has made over the last sixty years suggests little hope of peace in the Middle East ever being obtainable through politics alone.

- **1947 The Nation of Israel Is Born:** UN Resolution 181 recommended portioning the Palestine Mandate between Arabs and Jews. On May 14, 1948, Jewish leaders accepted the resolution even though their portion comprised only thirteen percent of the original and earlier Mandate and sixty percent of the land now being given to them was in the Negev desert.

- **1947-1948 Israel's War of Independence:** Arab leaders rejected the offer to create another Arab state in the Mandate; less than twenty-four hours after it had become a nation, Israel was invaded by the armies of Egypt, Syria, Transjordan, and Iraq. Miraculously, Israel's army defeated the attacks but in the fifteen months of war lost over 6,000 Israeli lives (in American terms, it would take *thirty-five* Vietnam memorials to reflect such a devastating loss of life – approximately one percent of their total population).

- **1949-1956 The Fedayeen Terrorist Raids**: Arab terrorists (fedayeen), trained and equipped by Egypt, repeatedly attacked Israeli civilians from bases in Lebanon,

Gaza, and Jordan. One thousand three hundred Israelis were killed or wounded in terrorist attacks.

- **1956 The Sinai/Suez War:** Egypt increased its fedayeen attacks, prevented Israeli shipping through the Suez Canal and blockaded the Israeli port of Eilat, violating international law and threatening Israel's economic survival. With the support of France and Britain, Israel captured the Sinai Peninsula and Gaza. Israel completely withdrew six months later when Egypt assured Israel unimpeded navigation and safety.

- **1959 Al Fatah Terrorist Raids:** Egyptian-born Yassar Arafat formed Fatah in 1959 to conduct guerrilla warfare against Israel. In 1965 Fatah adopted "the entanglement theory," which presumed that its repeated attacks would force Israel to respond aggressively against the Arab states hosting Arafat's fighters, thereby escalating the animosity between Israel and the Arab neighbors.

- **1964 Palestine Liberation Organization (PLO) Formed:** The PLO was formed in Egypt, supported by the Arab League as an umbrella organization for anti-Israel militant groups. In 1968, Arafat's Fatah joined the PLO and eventually dominated it. Over the decades, the PLO carried out thousands of attacks against Israelis and others around the world, including the first airplane hijackings.

- **1967 The Six-Day War:** Israel was forced to defend itself when Syria, Egypt, Jordan, and Iraq intensified their terrorist attacks. Egypt blocked the Israeli national waterways and expelled international observers. The four Arab countries mobilized more than 250,000 troops, armed with Soviet-supplied tanks and aircraft, on Israel's borders in preparation for a full-scale invasion. The Iraqi defense minister ordered his troops to "strike the enemy's civilian settlements, turn them into dust and pave the Arab roads with the skulls of Jews." Israel preempted them in a defensive war and managed to capture the West Bank from

Jordan, Gaza and the Sinai Peninsula from Egypt and the
Golan Heights from Syria.

- **1967 Resolution Adopted at the Arab Summit
  Conference in Khartoum:** "The Arab Heads of State have
  agreed to unite their political efforts at the international and
  diplomatic level to eliminate the effects of the aggression and
  to ensure the withdrawal of the aggressive Israeli forces from
  the Arab lands which have been occupied since the
  aggression of 5 June. This will be done within the framework
  of the main principles by which the Arab States abide,
  namely, no peace with Israel, no recognition of Israel, no
  negotiations with it, and insistence on the rights of the
  Palestinian people in their own country."

- **1967-1970 The War of Attrition:** Egyptian President
  Gamal Nasser ordered attacks on Israelis in the Sinai. During
  the three-year-long conflict, 1,424 Israeli soldiers and more
  than 100 Israeli civilians were killed.

- **1972 The Munich Massacre:** After 1967, Palestinian
  terrorists attacked Israelis worldwide. In their most public
  operation, the group Black September held hostage and
  murdered eleven members of the Israeli Olympic Team at the
  1972 Munich Olympics.

- **1973 The Yom Kippur War:** On October 6, 1973 – Yom
  Kippur, the holiest day in the Jewish calendar (and during
  the Muslim holy month of Ramadan) – Egypt and Syria
  opened a coordinated surprise attack against Israel. The
  equivalent of the total forces of NATO in Europe was
  mobilized on Israel's borders. On the Golan Heights,
  approximately 180 Israeli tanks faced an onslaught of 1,400
  Syrian tanks. Along the Suez Canal, fewer than 500 Israeli
  defenders with only three tanks were attacked by 600,000
  Egyptian soldiers, backed by 2,000 tanks and 550 aircraft.
  Caught unprepared, the IDF nonetheless managed to fend off
  this assault, cutting off Egyptian forces across the Suez Canal
  and pushing Syrian troops back from the Golan Heights.

While Israel was victorious militarily, the human toll was devastating – 2,688 Israeli soldiers were killed in the nearly three weeks of fighting.

Yom Kippur War and President Nixon

On October 6, 1973, Egypt and Syria, along with Iraqi troops, attacked Israel during Yom Kippur, the most holy day of the Jewish calendar. The Arab nations issued a warning that they would stop all oil shipments to any nation that assisted Israel in defense. Several days into the battle, the tiny nation of Israel was facing not only defeat but the real possibility of being "pushed into the sea" as her enemies had vowed. On October 9, Israeli Prime Minister Golda Meir made personal appeals to the leaders of the European nations. They each adamantly refused to help.

President Richard Nixon was wakened in the middle of the night by the ringing of his personal phone. Meir had absolutely no options left and made a passionate appeal for help. Nixon would later recall how he heard "his mother's voice" in the cry for help from the leader of the Jewish nation. Nixon's mother was a devout woman of prayer and would often read to him from the Scriptures. One day she told him "she had been given a dream" about his life. His mother explained in the dream she saw that "one day he would be in a position to save the Jewish people."

As soon as Prime Minister Meir finished speaking, President Nixon knew what he must do. From October 12th-14th, 1973, the United States shipped 22,325 tons of tanks, artillery, ammunition, and supplies to Israel and saved the Jewish nation from destruction.

"Against All Odds: Israel Survives." 2006 Documentary

- **1982-1985 The Lebanon Way:** After Jordan expelled the PLO in 1970 the terrorist organization entrenched itself in southern Lebanon. During Lebanon's ensuing civil war

(1975-1990), PLO attacks on northern Israel intensified. Israel entered Lebanon in 1982 to root out the terrorist group. The PLO was forced to relocate to Tunis. In 1985, Israel withdrew to a security zone approximately four miles wide along the border and stayed until it unilaterally withdrew in 2000.

By 1982, 95,000 people had already died in the bitter Lebanese civil war. During this war, Lebanese Christian Phalangists entered the Palestinian refugee camps of Sabra and Shatilla and massacred an estimated 460-700 people, including 200 PLO fighters. Although no Israelis were involved in the massacre, an Israeli court determined that Israel and General Ariel Sharon had indirect responsibility for it because the IDF did not stop the Phalangists' entry into the camps.

- **1987-1992 First Intifada:** The PLO initiated the Intifada ("shaking off") after false rumors of Israeli atrocities circulated through Palestinian territories. Palestinians claim this was a nonviolent uprising, but it quickly turned violent with twenty seven Israelis killed and more than 1,400 Israeli civilians and 1,700 Israeli soldiers injured. Almost half (1,000) of the Palestinian casualties were caused by other Palestinians in the "Intrafada" or internal, fighting among Palestinian factions.

- **1991 Persian Gulf War:** When the U.S.-led coalition fought to get Saddam Hussein out of Kuwait, Hussein attempted to draw Israel into the war and fired thirty-nine Scud missiles into Israel. To avoid disrupting the U.S.-led coalition, Israel did not retaliate.

- **1994 Suicide Bombings in Israel:** Eight civilians were killed in a suicide bombing on a bus in central Israel, a tactic that would increasingly be used by radical Islamic terrorist factions all over the world.

- **2000-2006 Second "Al-Aqsa" Intifada:** A campaign of suicide bombings and terrorist attacks began September 29,

2000, and within five years had left over 1,068 Israelis dead and over 7,000 injured – sixty-nine percent of them civilians. Approximately 3,000 Palestinians were also killed in this conflict.

- **2006 "Acts of War" against Israel:** After Israel completely withdrew from Gaza in 2005, Hamas and other terrorists unleashed a barrage of daily rocket attacks into Israel; within a six-month period after Israel's withdrawal, over 360 Qassam rockets hit the city of Sderot one mile away from Gaza. In June, 2006, terrorists from Gaza tunneled into Israel, killing two soldiers and kidnapping one. Two weeks later, Hezbollah, supported by Iran and Syria, attacked Israel across the internationally recognized Israeli-Lebanese border, killing eight soldiers and kidnapping two, simultaneously launching a barrage of rockets against civilian towns in northern Israel. Israel responded with a military operation that lasted thirty-four days. The conflict concluded with UN Resolution 1701, which went into effect on August 14, 2006. The UN hoped that a contingent of international troops would implement both Resolution 1701 and an earlier UN Resolution, 1559, which had also called for Hezbollah's disarmament.

Hezbollah refused to disarm or to free the three abducted Israeli soldiers until July 16, 2008, when the bodies of two of the soldiers were returned to Israel in an Israeli-Hezbollah swap for Lebanese prisoners. One abducted Israeli prisoner has yet to gain release.

This dire sixty year historic record must not be defined as Israel's battle for peace, but must be recognized as Israel's battle to survive. Life is the essential issue with God. And to this day, Israel continues to battle for its life.

Israel, America, and Politics

I had the privilege of sitting in the gallery of the House of Representatives while Israeli Prime Minister Olmert spoke to a joint session of Congress in 2006. This was his first visit to the U.S. as the

Prime Minister of Israel, and his address to our nation was the most sought-after ticketed event in Washington. Through the wonderful kindness (and contacts) of a dear Jewish friend, I was granted permission to attend.

I was seated in the upper section of the gallery, giving me a tremendous vantage point from which to observe the entire event taking place.

Every seat in the majestic and historic hall was filled. The Prime Minister entered to a standing ovation from the members of the Senate and Congress.

I include his opening comments and portions of the passionate and spiritual message he delivered on May 24, 2006:

> *Distinguished members of Congress, I come here – to the home of liberty and democracy – to tell you that my parents' dream, our dream, has only been partly fulfilled.*
>
> *We have succeeded in building a Jewish homeland. We have succeeded in creating an oasis of hope and opportunity in a troubled region.* ***But there has not yet been one year...one week...even one day...of peace in our tortured land.***
>
> *Over the past six years, more than 20,000 attempted terrorist attacks have been initiated against the people of Israel. Most, thankfully, have been foiled by our security forces. But, those which have succeeded have resulted in the deaths of hundreds of innocent civilians...and injury of thousands – many of the children guilty ONLY of being in what proved to be the wrong place at the wrong time.*
>
> *My parents Bella and Mordechai Olmert were lucky...They escaped the persecution in Ukraine and Russia and found sanctuary in Harbin, China. They immigrated to Israel to fulfill their dream of building a Jewish and democratic state living in peace in the land of our ancestors.*
>
> *My parents came to the Holy Land following a verse in the Old Testament in the book of Second Samuel: "I will appoint*

a place for my people Israel and I will plant them in their land and they will dwell in their own place and be disturbed no more."

For thousands of years, we Jews have been nourished and sustained by a yearning for our historic land. I, like many others, was raised with a deep conviction that the day would never come when we would have to relinquish parts of the land of our forefathers.

I believed, and to this day still believe, in our people's eternal and historic right to this entire land.

But I also believe that dreams alone will not quiet the guns that have fired unceasingly for nearly a hundred years. Dreams alone will not enable us to preserve a secure democratic Jewish state.

Jews all around the world read in this week's Torah portion: "And you will dwell in your land safely and I will give you peace in the land, and there shall be no cause for fear neither shall the sword cross through the Promised Land."

Painfully, we, the people of Israel, have learned to change our perspective. We have to compromise in the name of peace, to give up parts of our promised land in which every hill and valley is saturated with Jewish history and in which our heroes are buried. We have to relinquish part of our dream to leave room for the dream of others, so that all of us can enjoy a better future. For this painful but necessary task my government was elected.

And to this I am fully committed.

There were times during the Prime Minister's speech that emotionally felt like a Super Bowl due to the **outbursts of applause and numerous standing ovations** interrupting his powerful message. Sadly, the inability of everyone in the room to understand the Middle East dilemma was visually evident by an entire seating section declining to stand or applaud while the rest of the crowd unanimously did so.

I was not familiar with the seating arrangement of the chamber and asked the gentleman sitting next to me why this one area of the ground floor seemed so strangely opposed to everything Olmert had said.

"Democrats," he smirked.

"They are already posturing on the platform of a 'war-weary nation' for the presidential election in 2008," my gallery mate finished.

How could this entire segment of our nation's government become so defiant to simple truth? So much of the speech seemed to be just rational, non-partisan common sense to me. I admit my supreme political naiveté.

The remainder of the Prime Minister's words and the frozen indifference of the Democrat's Club seated directly below kept me mesmerized throughout the rest of the event.

Olmert warned our nation and the world as he spoke, "If we don't take Iran's bellicose rhetoric seriously now, we will be forced to take its nuclear aggression seriously later."

Thundering applause followed but the substantial slice of seats below sat stoically in slumbering silence.

At one point in his speech, the Prime Minster changed direction and stated, "Both our countries share a desire for energy security and prevention of global warming."

It was at this line in Olmert's amazing speech that a senior Democratic Congresswoman apparently woke up and began clapping wildly! And no one followed her lead.

No one.

I felt so badly for her. I really did.

She immediately stopped clapping, quickly glanced to her left and right, and forcing an awkward smile, slouched down in her chair.

Note to self: This really is "the big house," and when you bomb here, it hurts – bad.

The Prime Minister continued his speech:

We believe in the moral principles shared by our two nations, and they guide our political decisions.

We believe that life is sacred and fanaticism is not.

We believe that every democracy has the right and the duty to defend its citizens and its values against all enemies.

We believe that terrorism not only leads to war but that terrorism is war. A war that must be won every day. A war in which all men and women of goodwill must be allies.

We believe that peace among nations remains not just the noblest ideal but a genuine reality.

And then Prime Minister Olmert added to his list of "we believe" a statement he had spoken earlier. Perhaps prompted by the Spirit, he actually repeated the following sentence a second time, and it is not noted in the official transcript of his speech.

"And I still believe," the Prime Minister reiterated, "in our people's eternal and historic right to this entire land!"

Now try to understand.

This next event all happened in a nanosecond. At the moment Prime Minister Olmert finished repeating this last statement, I felt like the walls in the chamber of congress would cry out, "AMEN and AMEN" in response!

They didn't.

I sensed, certainly every single person at this historic meeting of both houses of Congress will burst out in applause.

And they didn't.

For some unknown reason, I then glanced down on the ground floor and my eyes were immediately drawn to the prominent Democratic Congresswoman again. It was possibly my imagination, but I swear she still looked crushed. She still seemed to be slouching in her chair and thinking that no one liked her and she had really bombed and she hated that, when she tried to get people to clap about global warming, no one helped her.

I couldn't take my eyes off of her!

"Well, too bad for her, buddy," a Jiminy Cricket conscience-like voice shattered my bleeding-heart trance.

"It's time for you to 'man-up' and do what's right in this house!" the thought echoed in my mind.

I happen to have really big hands, and perhaps they were created for just this moment in the history of the universe because all of a sudden, they just started clapping as loud and as fast as they could clap – all alone.

Maybe it was just going to be the Prime Minister of Israel and me, but at least everyone in the chambers would know that we agreed, "Dwelling in the land of Israel is the Jewish people's eternal and historic right!"

And then a wonderful thing happened.

The guy next to me joined in clapping, and then another person, and another, and another, and then the room exploded in applause!

And someday the entire world will join us.

Everyone Has an Opinion. No One Has a Solution.

As we left the historic hall and stepped outside there was a very large gathering of Jewish U.S. citizens protesting. They had hateful slogans on their angry signs against Olmert and his willingness to "negotiate land for peace."

I then saw another crowd gathering.

Christians.

They had a life-size mannequin of a Santa-Monica-surfer-looking Jesus.

(Man, I think He hates it when we do this kind of stuff.)

These Christians were also challenging Olmert on his right to give away the Land.

The arrogance.

I'm referring to the protestors, not the Prime Minister.

Things I Know and Don't Know

• I know by God's historic promise that it is the Jewish people's eternal and historic right to dwell in the land of Israel.

- I know God has put His Name uniquely upon the Jewish people and has made eternal promises to them that He will fulfill.

- I don't know if it is a wise choice to consolidate the Israeli settlements and continue building the security fence, or not.

- I do know the fence has saved hundreds of lives so far. If a fence would save the lives of my wife, son, daughter, family member, and friends, I know I would want them all to be living behind it.

- I don't know that dividing Jerusalem will bring any peace to the Jewish people in Israel and I know I am deeply distressed at the thought.

- I know there is no one who cares more about the welfare of Israelis than the citizens and leaders of Israel.

God Will Keep His Promises Concerning Israel

On May 15, 1948, the nation of Israel was born and Christian Zionists (along with many Jews) believed one of the promises of God concerning the Jews' return to Eretz Israel was being fulfilled. God has vested Himself by uniquely placing His Name upon the Jewish people.

Bringing them back to the land that He gave to their fathers is just the start of His wonderful restoration for them.

Ezekiel 36: 22-28:

Therefore say unto the house of Israel: Thus saith the Lord God: I do not this for your sake, O house of Israel, but for My holy name, which ye have profaned among the nations, whither ye came.

And I will sanctify My great name, which hath been profaned among the nations, which ye have profaned in the midst of them; and the nations shall know that I am HaShem, saith the Lord God, when I shall be sanctified in you before their eyes.

For I will take you from among the nations, and gather
you out of all the countries, and will bring you into your own
land. And I will sprinkle clean water upon you, and ye shall
be ¹clean; from all your uncleannesses, and from all your
idols, will I cleanse you.

A ²new heart also will I give you, and a ³new spirit will I
put within you; and I will take away the stony heart out of
your flesh, and I will give you a heart of flesh. And I will put
⁴My spirit within you, and cause you to walk in My statutes,
and ye shall keep Mine ordinances, and do them. And ye shall
dwell in the land that I gave to your fathers; and ye shall be
My people, and I will be your God.

When God has proven Himself holy among the Jewish people by
providing them ¹cleansing, ²new hearts, a ³new spirit, and by filling
them with ⁴His Spirit all the nations of the world will know the Lord
alone is God.

But right now we are somewhere in the process of the promise.

The nation of Israel is overwhelmingly secular. God has not yet
given the "house of Israel" the promised spiritual cleansing, or the new
spirit or the new heart, or filled them with His Spirit. Neither has He
given them all of the land He has promised to them. And until He does,
we believe whenever the Jews have attempted to take, or keep the
Promised Land apart from God's provision it has always been
disastrous for them.

Numbers 14:41-43:

Moses said, "Why do you transgress the word of
HaShem? It will not succeed. Do not ascend, for HaShem is
not in your midst! And do not be smitten before your
enemies. For the Amalekite and the Canaanite are there
before you, and you will fall by the sword, because you have
turned away from HaShem, and HaShem will not be with
you."

Deuteronomy 1: 42-44:

HaShem said to me: "Tell them, 'Do not ascend and do not do battle, for I am not among you; so that you not be struck down before your enemies.'" So I spoke to you, but you did not listen. You rebelled against the word of HaShem, and you were willful and climbed the mountain. The Amorite who dwell on that mountain went out against you and pursued you as the bees would do; they struck you in Seir until Hormah.

Answering the question:
"How are Christian Zionists trying to influence Israeli politics?"

Answer: "We aren't and we won't. We have great respect for Israel's national sovereignty and the democratic process that allows Israeli citizens to elect their leaders.

We will petition our state and national leaders to supply, support, and stand with Israel. We will also do everything we can to keep the U.S. government from enticing or intimidating Israel into making any concessions that Israel's leaders do not believe are in the best interests of their nation. We believe the continuation of blessings that have poured upon our nation are contingent upon our nation continuing to stand with the nation of Israel."

For my Christian readers:

The incomprehensible thought of having possibly over 50 million Christian supporters of Israel also carries for the Jewish mind the projection of the potential for unspeakable disaster for them. "What should happen in the years ahead if this enormous force for good becomes disenchanted with us?" Jewish observers ponder – possibly remembering the Christian support of Martin Luther.

"What might become of the free nation of Israel if Christian Zionists choose to negotiate their tourism and political support for 'favorable' decisions from key Israeli leaders?" some Jews must nervously and silently ask.

In light of our consistently heinous historic Christian testimony with the Jews, we must find a way to identify with the gravity of this question based on a Jewish perspective. Upon doing so, we Christians may be able to step down from our arrogant pedestals of assumption that lift us into really believing that we care more about the peace of Israel than their nation's elected leaders.

Question 7

"Do you really believe all the Jews are going to hell?"

Standard Christian Answer:
"Well, the Bible says..." a bunch of verses will follow along with "the Jesus talk."

Let me guess. You have picked up this book and rather than starting from the beginning you have turned to this chapter first.

Am I right?

For many Christians, the litmus test concerning the viability of one's "Christianosity" is not based on faith or love, but based on the ability to judge categorically who gets to go to heaven and who gets to go to hell. Thus, you may have turned to this chapter first, to see if the writer of this book is in fact a real Christian.

The Birds and the Bees and Faith

God is God, we are not, and He does not need to defend or explain his actions to us.

With that in mind, there are some very hard sayings God has given us in both the Hebrew Scriptures as well as in the New Testament that I sure wish He had explained in more detail.

My father once shared a "hard saying" with me.

On a Saturday afternoon, many, many years ago, my family was at the park having a picnic. (In a moment you will understand my need to make clear this happened not just many, but many, many years ago.)

My mother observed me laughing and pointing at the bizarre antics of a two-headed dog that was gyrating around the grassy area of the playground. Shortly after I was able to stop my hysterical laughing, I found myself all alone with my father, who appeared to have something very pressing on his mind.

"Victor," he hesitantly spoke my name.

"Yeah, Dad?" I hoped he would hurry as I was sure there were lots more funny things to see and do at the park.

"Your mother and I feel it is time I talk to you about 'the facts of life,'" he awkwardly continued.

"OK," I sighed, knowing this was probably going to take away at least five minutes of my day.

Well, as best I can remember, my dad finished up his entire presentation in about three minutes and concluded his fatherly presentation by asking if I had any questions.

"Nope!" I answered, trying to sound convincing as the fun-clock was still ticking.

"Alright then, my boy," my dad grinned, hugging me and swatting my rear end as I bounced off in search of adventure.

While watching his little boy walk away as a "young man," my father heard me remark to myself, "Man, I sure am glad humans don't do that."

"Open your Bibles, please," the preacher would now say. (I actually told this story on the very first Sunday I ever formally preached. Didn't get asked to preach again for a long time. A long, long, time.)

My point?

My father's "hard saying" concerning the facts of life (in my little boy world) was easily sloughed off, as I gleefully interpreted it as having nothing to do with me.

Hard Sayings in the Bible

There are hard sayings in the Torah:

Exodus 21:17:

One who curses his father or his mother shall surely be put to death.

We can all feel good about that one because none of us really believe God wants us to follow it! (apart from a few parents with rowdy teens who are reading this right now).

The New Testament also has many hard sayings, one of which is:

1 John 5:11-12:

And this is the testimony: God has given us eternal life, and this life is in his Son. He who has the Son has life; he who does not have the Son of God does not have life.

Central to Christian faith is the atoning death of Christ as the promised redeemer of mankind. Christians believe man is born into sin and can only be redeemed out of it.

The verses in I John are just several of many hard sayings regarding salvation that Christians unequivocally believe.

Sort of.

Sort of??

Well, yes.

Our community makes exclusions to the doctrine of "salvation through accepting Jesus" in a number of cases – especially when such doctrine would painfully touch our lives.

One exclusion in our Gospel message of "trusting in Jesus to be saved" theology has to do with the exception made for children getting into heaven.

You almost certainly will never hear a Christian pastor preach a sermon that suggests anything other than a merciful God welcoming the souls of deceased children into the everlasting.

Our Bible, however, gives no absolute teaching regarding the final resting place of babies and children. Some of the verses commonly used in attempts to find a concrete answer are:

Matthew 18:1-4:

At that time the disciples came to Jesus and asked, "Who is the greatest in the kingdom of heaven?"

He called a little child and had him stand among them. And he said: "I tell you the truth, unless you change and become like little children, you will never enter the kingdom of heaven. Therefore, whoever humbles himself like this child is the greatest in the kingdom of heaven."

Matthew 19:14:

Jesus said, "Let the little children come to me, and do not hinder them, for the kingdom of heaven belongs to such as these."

We add a few more verses and come up with a syllogistic conclusion that looks like this:

All kingdom members must become like children.
All children are childlike.
Therefore, all children are kingdom members.

This type of exegesis is frowned upon in any other portion of our Christian dogma, and is excluded in defining the very similar expression of God's loving desire found in the verses below.

1 Timothy 2:3-4:

This is good, and pleases God our Savior, who wants all men to be saved...

You will not find Christian theologians making the following syllogistic argument:

Our Savior is God.
God wants all men to be saved.
Therefore, all men shall be saved.

The defining of those things "God wants" in the above example will get you a very long explanation concerning the "three wills" of God: His sovereign decretive will, His preceptive will, and His will of disposition. I offer a very brief theological definition of each.

The three meanings of the will of God

(a) **Sovereign decretive will,** *the will by which God brings to pass whatsoever He decrees. This is hidden to us until it happens.*

(b) **Preceptive will** *is God's revealed law or commandments, which we have the power but not the right to break.*

(c) **Will of disposition** *describes God's attitude or disposition. It reveals what is pleasing to Him.*

R. C. Sproul. Essentials Truths of the Christian Faith. *Tyndale. 1992. pp. 67-69*

So, though God is pleased with the thought of all mankind being saved (c), apart from a "trusting in Jesus" experience (b), He only decrees (a) "saving" all children?

Yes.

This is exactly what most evangelical Protestant Christians believe to be true.

However, when it comes to adults actually receiving the gift of salvation through Christ, evangelicals have no such conformity in our beliefs.

- Some evangelicals believe you have no choice in choosing to believe in Christ: He chooses those whom He desires to be saved.

- And some evangelicals believe you have free will in making the decision to believe in Christ.

- Some evangelicals believe once you have been born again, you can, based on how you then behave, become un-born again and be eternally rejected by Christ.

- Yet some evangelicals believe once you have been born again, Jesus is pretty much stuck with you.
- Some Christian denominations perform infant baptisms.
- Some Christian denominations find the practice of infant baptism heretical.
- And almost every Christian will support the hope that children, under a certain unknown age, are deemed innocent by God.

"Innocent?"

My wife and I have raised four wonderful children and have two of the most divine grandchildren this world has ever seen, and I can tell you one thing for sure: All children (even ours) begin exhibiting the qualities of obstinate, self-centered little dictators as soon as they realize that crying could be taken to mean, "Pick me up now!"

The sinful tendencies of children become increasingly pronounced as these "innocents" enter their single-digit birthdays and learn to vocally express the apparent inborn mantra of "NO" and "MINE."

Any religious doctrine I may have had concocted concerning the "innocence of children" was dashed upon the harsh realities of actually raising mine.

The widely held Christian belief of mankind being born into sin seems much more likely to be true.

Squishy Christian Theology

This inconsistency regarding the absolution of children within the Christian doctrine of salvation through faith in Christ is essential to soothe our personal concerns regarding the eternal afterlife of the most precious of God's gifts: our children. And the reason we stretch and bend our theology so readily in the case of children is because the application of the doctrine touches our children.

To calm our need for answers concerning God's personal love for us, we have assumed an inferred doctrine called "the age of accountability." The teaching suggests that one who has not reached a certain level of maturity is not held accountable for his sins. Therefore, if he should die prior to reaching the "age of accountability," he will enter heaven based on the love and mercy of God.

In other words, he does not enter heaven based on faith in Jesus.

I have a brilliant friend, Pastor Frank Robinson, who is a theologian in the Wesleyan denomination. He perfectly states, "Determining the 'age of accountability' is a fairly squishy issue; always has been."

"It is not possible for babies and young children to make a saving faith decision regarding Jesus," we Christians assert.

"Therefore, it is not necessary for babies and young children to make a saving faith decision regarding Jesus to enter into the heavenly hereafter," we assume.

(Once again, this is an inferred doctrine, as there are no scriptures that state God has made special provision to grant deceased children automatic entrance into heaven.)

One might think the incongruence between our compassionate escape clause in our kid's salvation doctrine would wither when held next to the scorching proclamation found in New Testament "hard-saying" verses such as:

Romans 9:10-15:

Not only that, but Rebekah's children had one and the same father, our father, Isaac. Yet, before the twins were born or had done anything good or bad – in order that God's purpose in election might stand: not by works but by Him Who calls – she was told, "The older will serve the younger." Just as it is written: "Jacob I loved, but Esau I hated."

What then shall we say? Is God unjust? Not at all! For He says to Moses, "I will have mercy on whom I have mercy, and I will have compassion on whom I have compassion."

Even in the face of our own hard sayings such as these, we vehemently resist the possible Biblical truths conveyed by them. We find it easy to say, "God is God, and He doesn't have to explain Himself to us" except when His conduct might actually affect our lives in unfathomable ways.

Christians are left with no choice other than the porous "age of accountability" concept because the thought of our little ones being cast into hell by a loving God is absolutely irreconcilable with our perceived knowledge of His goodness.

For the record, I completely adhere to this non-canon of my faith. How can I do otherwise?

But should you ask many Christians about the absolute heavenly destiny of Muslim children who have perished; you will probably not receive the same assurance.

Standard Answer: "Well, we know that the Lord is good," or "The Lord looks upon the heart."

Should you ask about the eternity prepared for the babies and children of the Amalekites written about in the Hebrew Scriptures:

I Samuel 15:2-3:

Thus saith HaShem of hosts: "I remember that which Amalek did to Israel, how he set himself against him in the way, when he came up out of Egypt. Now go and smite Amalek, and utterly destroy all that they have, and spare them not; but slay both man and woman, infant and suckling, ox and sheep, camel and ass."

Standard Answer: "That was the Old Testament..."

You ask about that poor aborigine in the furthest parts of the outback who dies without ever having an opportunity to hear the Christian salvation message – the aborigine for whom "it is not possible to make a saving faith decision about Jesus, since he has never heard about Jesus!"

Standard Answer: "I'm not really sure about him, but let's talk about your salvation!"

And should a Jew be daring enough to ask a Christian about the resting place of the countless Jewish souls throughout the history of our faith who chose the option of a torturous death over a forced conversion to "trusting in Jesus."

Standard Answer: "The Bible says Jesus is the way, the truth and..." The Gospel preaching begins.

But should anyone ask about God's mercy and provision following the death of a baby within a Christian family:

Standard Answer: "Rest assured, he/she is in the bosom of Abraham and gazing into the eyes of Jesus!"

How can we Christians believe this way?

We must believe this way – but not because our Bible gives us clarity concerning the issue. We ultimately must believe this way because of the white-hot love we have for our children.

We ultimately must believe this way because of the intolerable contradictions we face when trying to reconcile a God of love with a God who would cast our children into eternal exile should they perish without a personal faith in Jesus.

Another exception many Christians hold dear regards adult members of our family who die without "confessing Jesus." In the heart-wrenching wrestling over loved ones who have passed on without publicly acknowledging a faith in Christ, many Christians find solace in the hope of a secret grace of God.

Perhaps He offers pardon one last time to the non-Christian relative through supernatural intervention in the very last nanoseconds of life.

Perhaps He does.

We just don't have any solid Scriptural teaching that would suggest this is the case, so we base our hope on His love – for those we love.

Unfortunately, you will seldom hear of Christians entertaining such a belief for the rest of humanity. The doctrine of our faith simply does not allow it, but the love in our heart for those we cherish – demands "the hope" for them.

The Jews and Redemption

At the Israeli Embassy in Los Angeles, my wife and I were to meet with the visiting Israeli Sephardi Chief Rabbi, Shlomo Amar. He is a striking, biblical-looking figure, every bit a member of the priesthood: dressed in flowing robes, crowned with a purple priestly mitre, his long, white beard engulfing most of his face, leaving only his tanned cheeks and gentle, full lips that smile in concert with his dark, dove-like eyes every time he finishes a sentence.

For my Christian readers:

Sephardim are one of the two major groups of Jewry. The word comes from the Hebrew *Sepharad*, originally the name of an area to which Jews were deported after the destruction of the First Temple. It was first used in the middle ages of the Jews of Spain; after the expulsion from Spain in 1492 the Sephardim settled in North Africa, Italy, Egypt, Palestine, Syria, the Balkans and the Turkish Empire.

Reprinted with permission from A Concise Encyclopedia of Judaism, by Dan Cohn – Sherbok. Oneworld Publications.

The rabbi spoke in Hebrew – whispered tones as his translator followed behind, addressing the small roomful of Jewish and Christian guests in English. At one point, while the rabbi took a quick break for a drink of water, our host, retired Israeli General Shimon Erem, stood up at the front of the room and turned around to face all of the guests.

"Now you know, when Mashiach comes, it is going to be just like this," he stated, instantly grabbing our attention.

"He too, will have a translator for all of you gentiles!" the General belly-laughed.

I think he might be right.

The rabbi finished speaking and thanked all of us for supporting the nation of Israel. He then graciously suggested he would like to answer as many questions as we had time to discuss.

The first guy to jump up was one of ours. Clutching an enormous black leather Bible (King James Red Letter Edition, I'm sure) he waved it around as he spoke.

"Rabbi?" he began.

My wife and I were already squirming. After being a pastor for so many years, you acquire a sixth sense when there is going to be a high cringe-factor moment.

"How do you Jews get forgiven from your sins, seeing that your temple was totally destroyed in 70 A.D and you no longer have any animal sacrifices?" the inquirer sneered.

For my Christian readers:

The Jewish people continue to mourn the loss of their Temple in Jerusalem. Most Conservative and Orthodox synagogues forbid the use of musical instruments during Shabbat services as a continuation of their ongoing sorrow. When speaking with a Jewish leader in my community, she compared the loss of the temple to the Jewish faith, to waking up one day and discovering the sun was gone. "How can we live? What can we tell our children?" she lamented. "Tisha B'Av" is one of the two major annual fast days in the Jewish faith, during which the entire community remembers and mourns the destruction of the Temple.

This Christian Zionist had no interest whatsoever in Jewish theology concerning sin and redemption. His naive mind offered not a question, but a trap – a perfect "gotcha!" moment.

No temple + no sacrifices = no forgiveness of sin.

Merciful God.

The rude abrasiveness of our Christian soldiers.

This short (thank the Lord!) and naive confrontation with such an honored rabbi is a classic example of a pro-Israel Christian and lover of the Jewish people who does not have a single, cherished Jewish friend.

Rabbi Amar certainly had more grace for the loaded question than

I (obviously) did, as he smiled and offered a brief and sincere answer.

My Torah-loving Jewish friends are very aware of their sinfulness before God, and this is not the first time in history they have endured without having their Temple and sacrificial offerings.

Christians should remember that after the destruction of the first Temple and during the Babylonian exile, faithful Jewish people continued in the covenantal relationship with the Almighty – and He with them.

Leviticus 26:44:

But despite all this, while they will be I the land of their enemies, I will not have been revolted by them nor will I have rejected them to obliterate them, to annul My covenant with them – for I am HaShem, their God.

Since the destruction of their second Temple and the inability to offer the necessary sacrifices for sin, Jews believe God has made provision for them as He speaks through the Scriptures.

Hosea 6:6:

For I desire mercy, and not sacrifice, and the knowledge of God rather than burnt-offerings.

Micah 6:7-8:

Will HaShem be pleased with thousands of rams, with ten thousands of rivers of oil? Shall I give my first-born for my transgression, the fruit of my body for the sin of my soul?' It hath been told thee, O man, what is good, and what HaShem doth require of thee: only to do justly, and to love mercy, and to walk humbly with thy God.

Yom Kippur –

"Day of Atonement," taken from the commands in Leviticus 16.

Leviticus 16:29-34:

This shall remain for you *an eternal decree: In the seventh month, on the tenth of the month, you shall afflict yourselves and you shall not do any work, neither the native nor the proselyte who dwells among you. For on this day he shall provide atonement for you to cleanse you; from all your sins before HaShem shall you be cleansed.*

It is a Sabbath of complete rest for you, and you shall afflict yourselves; an eternal decree.

The Kohen or High Priest, who has been anointed or who has been given the authority to serve in place of his father, shall provide atonement; he shall don the linen vestments, the sacred vestments. He shall bring atonement upon the Holy of Holies, and he shall bring atonement upon the Tent of Meeting and the Altar; and upon the Kohanim and upon all the people of the congregation shall he bring atonement. This shall be to you an eternal decree to bring atonement upon the Children of Israel for all their sins once a year; and (Aaron) did as HaShem commanded Moses.

As noted, it is an eternal statute for the Jews, to be performed once a year. It is a day set aside to afflict the soul, to atone for the sins of the past year, but only regarding sins against God.

In Jewish belief, though sins against your fellow man are confessed to the Almighty, they can only be truly forgiven by repentance and restitution toward the one you have sinned against.

My wife and I attended Yom Kippur at the beautiful Mosaic Law conservative synagogue in Sacramento, California. Greeted by one of our dearest Jewish friends, he invited us to sit with him. As the service began, he became our spiritual guide through the next 2-1/2 hours of psalms, prayers, and repentance.

Yom Kippur begins each year with the prayer, *Kol Nidre*, meaning "for all the vows or pledges." This opening prayer, on the most holy

Jewish holiday, seeks forgiveness for any rash vows that are made to the Almighty in the year to come. The *Kol Nidre* was in use as early as the 8th century, and considered originally a means of annulling oaths forced on Jews by their Christian persecutors.

Upon hearing the history and original purpose of this ancient prayer, my wife and I silently wept.

For my Christian readers:

If you have never attended a Yom Kippur service, I strongly recommend you ask permission to do so from a Jewish friend or rabbi. You will find it to be an incredibly intimate and probing spiritual experience. I wish our Christian community had an equivalent expression in our sacraments. The brevity with which we observe our Christian Communion is often unworthy of the seriousness of our transgression and beliefs concerning the cost of our redemption.

A Rabbi Explains To Me

Rabbi Matt Friedman, of Sacramento, CA, explained to me:

One of the greatest differences between Judaism and Christianity is the belief that the death of Jesus served as everlasting reconciliation for those who accepted him as savior. Jesus's death provided his followers the sacrificial offering that cleansed his followers of sin and guaranteed them eternal life after death.

These beliefs are not surprising considering the Biblical history of atonement of sins through animal sacrifices and the Christian belief of Jesus as being God incarnate on earth. If the sacrifice of an animal, which is of lower stature than a human, can bring atonement, then the sacrifice of Jesus, who was God incarnate, could bring about a salvation far beyond that which had been considered before. It is at this point that a crucial difference between Judaism and Christianity becomes apparent both theologically and historically.

*Judaism does not accept the key theological viewpoints that
God would appear incarnate on earth, the messiah would
have divine origins or that the offering of a human was
either allowable or efficacious for the atonement of sins for
other humans.*

A Rabbi Asks Me

I flew into NY at the invitation of AIPAC for an event in Connecticut along with author David Brog. David and I were joined by AIPAC's Jeff Mendelsohn, who would moderate our panel discussion called 'Friends of the Faith,' which we have now presented before hundreds of Jewish attendees around the nation.

All three of us gasped as our chauffeur pulled up to the exclusive Connecticut gated community and entered the circular driveway framing the front of the enormous and stately mansion where the evening event was being held. There was a long row of young men in white tuxedos parking cars as the guests arrived.

Over 200 people had gathered in the backyard "garden of Eden" (one rabbi exclaimed) as gourmet food and wine stations offered the finest culinary treats.

The gracious host family requested that everyone be seated in the staging area as our panel stepped onto a stage equipped with three large director's chairs and hand-held microphones. After some very kind introductions, we were off!

Jeff asked David Brog, "Exactly who are these evangelical Christians...and what do they believe?" David always brings me to tears as he shares (with his amazing intellect and Ivy League education) the basics of the Christian faith, including our belief in the Word of God and divinity of Jesus Christ. David Brog is a "Jewish Jew for Judaism," as he explains it. Though he understands Christian theology, he does not share in our beliefs contained within it.

I felt a responsibility to revisit Christianity's abominable history of persecuting the Jews, after which I asked forgiveness for the 2,000 years of wickedness the Jews have suffered from those who have carried our banner.

I attempted to explain to the audience why, today, evangelical Christians feel it is an honor, a blessing, a privilege, and a commandment for us to love and support the Jewish community and those in the land of Israel.

For many in attendance at these events, it is the very first time they have heard of such things.

At the conclusion of the evening, a handsome young orthodox rabbi approached me. As we shook hands, he held mine with both of his and thanked me for the words I had spoken.

Looking directly into my face, he then asked, "Pastor, as a Christian, you believe we did not recognize Mashiach when He came. In considering that, where do you believe the Jews now are as a people?"

"Rabbi, first of all, thank you for allowing me to be here tonight and for believing my words were sincere," I answered.

I clumsily began, "There is a Pharisee mentioned in the New Testament, whose name is Saul." (Saul was a Jewish Pharisee who upon believing in Jesus as Messiah became the Apostle Paul of the New Testament.)

"I'm familiar with the writings of Paul," he smiled.

I was so busted!

I could feel my face flush with embarrassment from my clever bridge-building attempts, but the rabbi's appreciative grin quickly released me from my ignorance.

"Well, first of all," I tried again, "HaShem has been God for a long time, is very good at it, and He knows all things before they happen."

"It was no shock to Him," I continued, "that most of Israel did not recognize Jesus as Mashiach."

"And, as you know, rabbi, it's not like you guys were all that nice to some of the prophets HaShem sent your way," I added, while carefully smiling.

The rabbi gave a little laugh and nodded his head, "No, we sure weren't."

"The mystery of gentile inclusion into the mercies of God is written in Torah and the writings," I suggested as I quoted one brief example:

O praise the Lord all you gentiles, laud Him all you peoples.

For the mercy of the Lord toward us is great!

Psalm 117:1-2.

"We believe, as written in the book of Romans, that, because the nation of Israel did not recognize Jesus as their Messiah, God has 'grafted in' the gentiles who do believe in Him into the Abrahamic Covenant.

It is an unnatural grafting," I continued, "as we are wild branches and yet have been made part of a 'good olive tree.'"

"This next part of my Christian theology is very embarrassing for me to talk about," I confided to the rabbi.

"Why is that?" he asked.

"Our writings teach that some of the natural branches, the Jews, were temporarily broken off. They were broken off so that gentiles could be grafted in to the promises that were exclusively given to the Jews." I reiterated.

"The writing then states we were grafted in so that the nation of Israel might become envious, and return to her God," I summarized.

"In our 2,000-year history, envy is not one of the emotions Christianity has provoked within the hearts of Jews," I sadly confessed.

"But you see this as a paternal act of God toward us?" the rabbi earnestly asked.

"I do," I quickly answered, "because it is. You are His first-born!"

"I am very familiar with the chapters in Romans you are speaking about, and will read them again tonight," my new friend smiled as he shook my hand once again.

Answering the question:
"Do you really believe all the Jews are going to hell?"

Answer: Christian theology teaches that the final redemption for Israel and the gentiles is revealed through the coming of Messiah, a belief many rabbis teach as well. (Upon Messiah's arrival, we can ask if it is His first or second visit!)

Christians have searched the Hebrew Scriptures and New Testament, and have come to believe Jesus fulfilled every Messianic prophecy concerning the foretold suffering of Messiah, and upon His return, will fulfill those of the promised victorious Messiah as well.

We believe God has allowed what we perceive regarding Messiah to remain hidden from the Jews in order that the gentiles might be "grafted in" to the mercies of God.

The New Testament also teaches "salvation has come to the gentiles to make Israel envious." Though it makes no sense to me, and is humiliating to say we believe this in light of our appalling history with the Jewish people, nonetheless, it is written in our Scriptures.

I believe the Almighty uniquely loves the Jewish people, and I believe He has made them many eternal promises – redemption for "all of Israel" being one of them.

I don't understand how God is going to bring all of these pieces of my faith together; but I believe He will, and I believe as it is written: "all of Israel will be saved."

Romans 11:25-27:

For I do not desire, brethren, that you should be ignorant of this mystery, lest you should be wise in your own opinion, that blindness in part has happened to Israel until the fullness of the gentiles has come in. And so all Israel will be saved, as it is written: "The Deliverer will come out of Zion, and He will turn away ungodliness from Jacob; for this is My covenant with them, when I take away their sins" (Isaiah 59:20-21).

Question 8

"You love your enemies? How can you love the terrorists that are killing our children in Israel?"

Standard Christian Answer:
"Jesus taught us to love our enemies, and so we 'hate the sin but love the sinner'" and the "Jesus talk" begins.

I was invited to speak at a university during their campus Israel Week. Part way through my presentation, I noticed two female Jewish students in an animated, whispered exchange. As I looked their way, our eyes met for just a moment, and both of them immediately raised their hands into the air.

"Pastor Victor?" one of them spoke as I acknowledged them both.

"You just said that you live within a Sunni Muslim community and you love your neighbors?" she accurately restated my comments.

"How can you say you love the Jews, and also love the hate-filled terrorists that are killing our children in Israel?" she sternly challenged my apparent insincerity.

"Hang on a minute, sister!" I pleaded as I considered her heartrending question.

"You are talking about two completely different situations here. The militant men and women who are killing people in Israel and around the world are nothing like the people I live among in Sacramento," I began.

Love Your Neighbor as You Love Yourself

My family and I have lived within a Sunni Muslim community in our neighborhood for over a decade. Among my Christian friends, very few of them have a Muslim friend.

As a result, I often find myself a lone voice defending the observant, peace-loving Muslim faith community. Even some of the most outspoken of Christian ex-Muslims seem to have only experienced a hate-filled expression of Islam and often whip the sheep of our Christian flocks into a lather with their shrill stereotyping of all Muslims.

I have such great concern for the Christian community and our proclivity to hate.

Let's be honest.

Though there are stellar examples among individuals and some local churches, Christianity is not known for loving. We are not known for loving gays, bisexuals, or transsexuals. We are not known for loving Jehovah's Witnesses, Mormons, and Muslims. Sadly, at this point in history Christians are not even known for loving one another all that much.

I received a phone call from an outstanding Christian defender of Israel. With tears, she pleaded with me to "immediately sell your house and move!"

She was so convinced my Muslim neighbors were just waiting for the right moment to decapitate my entire family, this friend and Christian Zionist could not rest until she contacted me.

She doesn't have one close Muslim friend and she has never met nor does she know any of my neighbors.

My Wonderful Muslim Neighbors

Tiny voices yelling "Vectorrr, Vectorrrr!" from 2- and-3-year-old Muslim children next door fill my ears and heart with joy every time I walk past them. They shout it out with such pure glee! Until they reach elementary school age, we are the only non-Muslim people most of these little ones will ever know – and my name is often the first American name they learn.

Their mothers grin and wave to my wife and me as they chatter to each other in Urdu, whenever we pass by their homes on one of our early evening neighborhood walks

The older adolescent brothers (and sometimes sisters) are at our front door nearly every day asking, "Can we play in the 'Teen Center'?" (We have lived in the inner city for the last twenty-two years and have always reached out to the kids in our neighborhood. To better touch their lives, we built a Teen Center hangout in our backyard. It has become a "Starbucks-Bible study-movie night-slumber party-birthday party-pro-Israel gathering-study hall-video game arcade-Nachos Night-Sunni Muslim 'clubhouse'"!)

Numerous times I have been asked to bring the Muslim boys to the hospital in emergency situations. Twice I have had to sign my name as a family member (their "Uncle Victor") so they could receive emergency stitches and tetanus shots needed. We still laugh about it!

My wife has taxied and assisted many of the Muslim women in the community with their doctor's visits and children's school registration appointments.

On Christmas, we give gifts to each of the children, and last year we were able to give beautiful handmade baby blankets to each of the (always many!) pregnant mothers.

Aziz lives a few homes down from us and his door-less garage is our local *Madrasa*.

I have spent hours over the years talking with their community leaders: Aziz, and Mohammad, and Mohammad, and Hyder, and Habidur, and Mohammad about their faith in Allah. Through over a decade of personal relationships with these neighbors, I have intimately watched, listened and learned firsthand about their practice of Sunni, Muslim faith.

They speak of Allah as "always kind and merciful."

The Muslim mothers and fathers dote over their children and grandchildren as we do ours.

They respect our family deeply and because they have observed our faith as sincere, they believe we will convert to the Muslim faith when "Jesus returns to rule over the earth."

Not the Jewish Jesus of the New Testament.

> "The Prophet said: 'There is no prophet between me and him, that is, Jesus. He will destroy the Antichrist and will live on the earth for forty years and then he will die. The Muslims will pray over him.'" Sunan Abu Dawood, Book 37, Number 4310. Narrated by AbuHurayrah.
>
> "After his descention (sic) on earth, Jesus will marry. He will have children, and he will remain on the earth 19 years after marriage. He will pass away and Muslims will perform his Funeral Prayer and bury him next to the Prophet Muhammad." Tirmidhi, as quoted by Mufti A.H. Elias. Jesus (Isa) A.S. in Islam, and his Second Coming. in http://www.islam.tc/prophecies/jesus.html

The thoughts of jihad as expressed through militant Islam are abhorrent to them. They view all acts of terrorism committed by people claiming to be followers of Islam as political and an abomination to the Quran and the true teachings of Islam.

When asked about the violence in the Quran commanded by Allah against infidels, my Muslim neighbors explained their convictions concerning those passages. They believe the commands were of ancient times and only against specific people of those times.

Our Violent Scriptures

Our Jewish/Christian scriptures are historically violent. We are all familiar with that old campfire favorite, Psalm 137.

Psalm 137:8-9:

> O daughter of Babylon, that art to be destroyed; happy shall he be, that repayeth thee as thou hast served us. Happy

*shall he be, that taketh and dasheth thy little ones against
the rock.*

We learn about the Jewish prophet Samuel as he executes God's
vengeance toward the gentile king, Agag.

1 Samuel 15:33:

*And Samuel said: As thy sword hath made women
childless, so shall thy mother be childless among women.
And Samuel hewed Agag in pieces before HaShem in Gilgal.*

And there is Moses challenging the Israeli officers concerning the
guidelines of their holy war.

Numbers 31:15-18:

*Moses said to them, "Did you let every female live?
Behold – they caused the Children of Israel, by the word of
Balaam, to commit a betrayal against HaShem regarding
the matter of Peor; and the plague occurred in the assembly
of HaShem. So now, kill every male among the young
children, and every woman fit to know a man by lying with
a male, you shall kill. But all the young girls among the
women who have not known lying with a male, you may
keep alive for yourselves."*

These are just a few of the many examples of bloodshed and
violence in the name of God found within our scriptures.

Speaking Out Against Religious Violence

I have been angrily challenged by a number of friends, "If your
Muslim neighbors don't agree with the militant Islamic movement,
then why don't they speak out against it?"

I answer with, "Why didn't one single U.S. newspaper print one
single Islamic cartoon out of the twelve published in 2006 by the

Danish newspaper, *Jyllands-Posten?*"[6]

Many of our most powerful and protected American institutions of free speech, our daily newspapers, claimed they would not print the satirical cartoons out of "respect" for Islam. None of our television entertainment/news stations showed any of the illustrations, citing the same hollow reasoning.

A nice gesture. If only these same organizations had a track record of showing respect toward Jewish or Christian sensibilities.

I canceled my subscription to our local paper after the editor wasted a half-page of good ink defending the paper's reasons for not printing the drawings. In his pontification about tolerance toward all religious views, not once did the editor of The *Sacramento Bee* (or the editors of any national paper I read) mention fear of reprisal from militant Islamic fundamentalists as the real reason for the newspaper's restraint.

How transparently dishonest, cowardly, and, perhaps – smart of them.

Until the most influential voices in America find the honesty and courage to fully confront the hate-filled enemies of Israel (and the world), why would I demand or expect the neighbors on my block to lead the way?

Pigs and Monkeys?

When talking with my neighbors about the teachings of the Quran referring to Jews as "pigs and monkeys," they acknowledge these verses exist. They, like many Muslims believe they relate to a time in Israel's history when the Jews were rebelling against God and rejecting the

---

[6] The *Jyllands-Posten* Muhammad cartoon rioting resulted from the printing of 12 editorial cartoons, most of which depicted the Islamic prophet Muhammed in the Danish newspaper, *Jyllands-Posten* on September 30, 2005. Protests erupted across the Muslim world, some of which became violent, with police firing on the crowds (resulting in more than 100 deaths). Outraged Muslim crowds set fire to the Danish Embassies in Syria, Lebanon, and Iran, stormed European buildings, and desecrated the Danish, Dutch, Norwegian, and German flags in Gaza City. While a number of Muslim leaders called for protesters to remain peaceful, other Muslim leaders around the world, including Mahmoud al-Zahar of Hamas, issued death threats.

words of their prophets. It is during these times, they believe, Allah referred to certain Sabbath breaking Jews as "monkeys and pigs:"

Suras 2:66 Quran:

And well ye knew those amongst you who transgressed in the matter of the Sabbath: We said to them: "Be ye apes, despised and rejected."

Suras 5:60 Quran:.

Say: "Shall I point out to you something much worse than this, (as judged) by the treatment it received from Allah? Those who incurred the curse of Allah and His wrath, those of whom some He transformed into apes and swine, those who worshipped evil; these are (many times) worse in rank, and far more astray from the even path!"

Suras 7:166 Quran:

When in their insolence they transgressed (all) prohibitions, We said to them: "Be ye apes, despised and rejected."

Let's not forget the writings of the Jewish prophet Jeremiah, and the name-calling he employed toward the Children of Israel in a time of their rebellion:

Jeremiah 2:24:

...thou art a swift young camel traversing her ways; a wild ass used to the wilderness, that snuffeth up the wind in her desire; her lust, who can hinder it? All they that seek her will not weary themselves; in her month they shall find her.

Camels and wild donkeys – in heat?
Yikes!

Makes "pigs and monkeys" sound almost cute in comparison.

Diversity within Islam

The cover of the *Smithsonian Magazine*, December 2008, asks: "THE SUFI QUESTION: Can the joyous Muslim movement counter the forces of radical extremism?"

The incredibly wide spectrum of Islamic faith expression is as broad and diverse as are the Jewish and Christian manifestations of belief.

> ### *According to Raziana Soobratty writing in* *PeopleOfFaith.org.uk*
>
> *"Muhammad predicted that his followers would be divided into seventy-three sects, every one of whom would go to hell, except for one sect, the religion professed by himself and his companions. However, the number of Islamic sects – now over 150 – has far exceeded Muhammad's prediction."*

Almost none of my Christian friends have any life experience with Muslims other than observing the militant ones reported on by CNN and FOX news stations.

Having said all of the above, I am well aware of the clear and present danger facing the nation of Israel and the rest of the world from the hate-filled proponents of militant Islam. The Muslim Brotherhood, Hamas, Fatah, Al-Qaeda, and Hezbollah are just a few of the Islamic religious sects calling for the destruction of the nation of Israel.

Israel's Hate-Filled Enemies

The Muslim Brotherhood

From the 1928 Charter of the Muslim Brotherhood: "Allah is its target, the Prophet is its model, the Quran is its Constitution; Jihad is its path, and death for the sake of Allah is the loftiest of its wishes."

> *Founded in 1928 by the Egyptian activist Hasan al-Banna, the Sunni Muslim Brotherhood is one of the oldest, largest, and most influential Islamist organizations.*

Egypt has historically been the center of the Brotherhood's operations, though the group maintains offshoots throughout the Arab-Muslim world, including in Afghanistan, Bahrain, Iran, Iraq, Jordan, the Palestinian territories (Hamas), Saudi Arabia, Syria, and Sudan and is also active in the United States and Europe.

Islam expert Robert Spencer has called the Muslim Brotherhood, the parent organization of Hamas and al Qaeda.

The Brotherhood was founded in accordance with al-Banna's proclamation that Islam be "given supremacy over all matters of life." Accordingly, the Brotherhood seeks to establish an Islamic Caliphate (a central ruling office of Islam) spanning the entire Muslim world. It also aspires to make Islamic (Sharia) law the sole basis of jurisprudence and governance. Toward this purpose – encapsulated in the Brotherhood's militant credo is: "God is our objective, the Koran is our Constitution, the Prophet is our leader, struggle is our way, and death for the sake of God is the highest of our aspirations." The Brotherhood since its founding has supported the use of armed struggle, or jihad.

The Brotherhood supports the waging of jihad against non-Muslim infidels, and has expressed support for terrorism against Israel, whose legitimacy the Brotherhood does not recognize, and against the West, particularly the United States.

Discoverthenetwork.org

www.discoverthenetworks.org/groupProfile.asp?grpidc8

Hamas

Hamas is one of the largest and most influential Palestinian militant movements. In January, 2006, they won the Palestinian Authority's (PA) general legislative elections by defeating Fatah, the party of the PA's president, Mahmoud Abbas, and setting the stage for the power struggle that ended with Hamas's violent takeover of Gaza.

The principles of Hamas are stated in their charter. Following are highlights: The introduction to the charter quotes the founder of the Egyptian Muslim Brotherhood, Hassan al-Banna, as saying: "Israel will continue to exist until Islam will obliterate it, just as it obliterated others before it."

The Charter of Allah

The Platform of the Islamic Resistance Movement, (HAMAS)

Article 13: "*Initiatives, and so-called peaceful solutions and international conferences, are in contradiction to the principles of the Islamic Resistance Movement. Now and then the call goes out for the convening of an international conference to look for ways of solving the (Palestinian) question. There is no solution to the Palestinian question except by Jihad. All initiatives, proposals, and International Conferences are all a waste of time and vain endeavors.*"

Article 31: "*Under the wing of Islam, it is possible for the followers of the three religions – Islam, Christianity and Judaism – to coexist in peace and quiet with each other. Peace and quiet would not be possible except under the wing of Islam. Past and present history are the best witness to that. It is the duty of the followers of other religions to stop disputing the sovereignty of Islam in this region, because the day these followers should take over there will be nothing but carnage, displacement and terror. Every one of them is at variance with his fellow religionists, not to speak about followers of other religionists. Past and present history are full of examples to prove this fact.*"

(Muslim Brotherhood Charter. *1928*)

Palestine Liberation Organization, (PLO)

The rebirth of Israel in 1948 and the ensuing wars between Israel and Arab nations profoundly changed the boundaries of Israel as wars between nations do. Founded in 1964 as an organization to demand a Palestinian state, the PLO grew in regional and international prominence after Arab armies proved unable to defeat Israel in the Six-Day War of 1967, and Israel reclaimed the Gaza Strip and West Bank.

For my Christian readers:

In the 2nd century C.E., the Roman emperor Hadrian renamed the land of Judah, Palestine, after the extinct people and enemies of Israel, the Philistines. In recent history, the term "Palestinian" was viewed by Arabs living in Palestine as a derogatory colonialist British term, designed to erase their Arab identity. The Arabs living in Palestine never had a separate state and simply saw themselves as part of the larger Arab or Muslim community. It was Yasser Arafat who began using the term "Palestinian" in 1964 to describe the Arabs living in Israel and their national identity.

There is no such country as Palestine. "Palestine" is a term the Zionists invented. There is no Palestine in the Bible. Our country was, for centuries, part of Syria. "Palestine" is alien to us. It is the Zionists who introduced it.

Auni Bey Abdul-Hadi, Syrian Arab leader to British Peel Commission, 1937

In 1993, Israeli officials led by Prime Minister Yitzhak Rabin and Palestinian leaders from the Palestine Liberation Organization directed by Yasser Arafat, attempted to find a peaceful solution to the ongoing terrorist attacks upon Israel. These series of meetings became known as the Oslo Peace Process. An extraordinary moment during these talks came as the content of letters written by Yasser Arafat accepting Israel's right to exist was made known to the world.

LETTER FROM YASSER ARAFAT TO PRIME MINISTER RABIN:

From: The Jewish Virtual Library (www.jewishvirtuallibrary.org/jsource/Peace/recogn.html)

September 9, 1993
Yitzhak Rabin
Prime Minister of Israel

Mr. Prime Minister,

The signing of the Declaration of Principles marks a new era in the history of the Middle East. In firm conviction thereof, I would like to confirm the following PLO commitments:

The PLO recognizes the right of the State of Israel to exist in peace and security.

The PLO accepts United Nations Security Council Resolutions 242 and 338.

The PLO commits itself to the Middle East peace process, and to a peaceful resolution of the conflict between the two sides and declares that all outstanding issues relating to permanent status will be resolved through negotiations.

The PLO considers that the signing of the Declaration of Principles constitutes a historic event, inaugurating a new epoch of peaceful coexistence, free from violence and all other acts which endanger peace and stability. Accordingly, the PLO renounces the use of terrorism and other acts of violence and will assume responsibility over all PLO elements and personnel in order to assure their compliance, prevent violations and discipline violators.

In view of the promise of a new era and the signing of the Declaration of Principles and based on Palestinian acceptance of Security Council Resolutions 242 and 338, the PLO affirms that those articles of the Palestinian Covenant which deny Israel's right to exist, and the provisions of the

Covenant which are inconsistent with the commitments of this letter are now inoperative and no longer valid. Consequently, the PLO undertakes to submit to the Palestinian National Council for formal approval the necessary changes in regard to the Palestinian Covenant.

Sincerely,
Yasser Arafat
Chairman
The Palestine Liberation Organization

LETTER FROM YASSER ARAFAT TO NORWEGIAN FOREIGN MINISTER:

September 9, 1993
His Excellency
Johan Jorgen Holst
Foreign Minister of Norway

Dear Minister Holst,

I would like to confirm to you that, upon the signing of the Declaration of Principles, the PLO encourages and calls upon the Palestinian people in the West Bank and Gaza Strip to take part in the steps leading to the normalization of life, rejecting violence and terrorism, contributing to peace and stability and participating actively in shaping reconstruction, economic development and cooperation.

Sincerely,
Yasser Arafat
Chairman
The Palestine Liberation Organization

LETTER FROM PRIME MINISTER RABIN TO YASSER ARAFAT:

September 9, 1993
Yasser Arafat
Chairman
The Palestinian Liberation Organization

Mr. Chairman,

In response to your letter of September 9, 1993, I wish to confirm to you that, in light of the PLO commitments included in your letter, the Government of Israel has decided to recognize the PLO as the representative of the Palestinian people and commence negotiations with the PLO within the Middle East peace process.

Yitzhak Rabin
Prime Minister of Israel

The discovery of these love notes being passed between sworn enemies filled many weary and wary hearts with hopes for peace in the land of Israel. However, now fifteen years later and after numerous promises to do so, the PLO has never changed its Palestinian National Charter, which calls for the destruction of the nation of Israel.

Arafat Aide Admits PLO Charter Never Altered After Oslo Accords.
World Net Daily Staff. "Still Calling for Israel's Destruction" *World Net Daily*, October 10, 2002.

Shortly after Oslo II was passed in the Knesset, Rabin decided on a public campaign to rally his supporters, and it was following the first such rally in Tel Aviv in November 1995, that he was assassinated by a Jewish religious fanatic opposed to the peace process. Israelis were horrified, and after a funeral attended by many international leaders, including Arabs, a round of soul-searching and recriminations began.

One of the unanimous agreements reached in the 1993 Oslo Accords required removal of the many clauses within the Palestinian National Charter calling for violence and the destruction of Israel. Though there has been much debate as to the sincerity of Arafat's convictions concerning Israel's right to exist, to this day, the rewriting of the Palestinian National Charter has never been accomplished, and a new one was never proposed.

In early October 2002, the Dubai newspaper *Al Bayan* quoted Arafat's Foreign Minister Farouk Kaddoumi as admitting that the PLO National Covenant has never been changed.

Portions of the Present Palestinian National Charter

Article 1: Palestine is the homeland of the Arab Palestinian people; it is an indivisible part of the Arab homeland, and the Palestinian people are an integral part of the Arab nation.

Article 3: The Palestinian Arab people possess the legal right to their homeland and have the right to determine their destiny after achieving the liberation of their country in accordance with their wishes and entirely of their own accord and will.

Article 6: The Jews who had normally resided in Palestine until the beginning of the Zionist invasion will be considered Palestinians.

Article 9: Armed struggle is the only way to liberate Palestine. Thus it is the overall strategy, not merely a tactical phase. The Palestinian Arab people assert their absolute determination and firm resolution to continue their armed struggle and to work for an armed popular revolution for the liberation of their country and their return to it. They also assert their right to normal life in Palestine and to exercise their right to self-determination and sovereignty over it.

Article 15: The liberation of Palestine, from an Arab viewpoint, is a national (qawmi) duty and it attempts to repel the Zionist and imperialist aggression against the Arab homeland, and aims at the elimination of Zionism in Palestine. Absolute responsibility for this falls upon the Arab nation – peoples and governments – with the Arab people of Palestine in the vanguard. Accordingly, the Arab nation must mobilize all its military, human, moral, and spiritual capabilities to participate actively with the Palestinian people in the liberation of Palestine. It must, particularly in the phase of the armed Palestinian revolution, offer and furnish the Palestinian people with all possible help, and material and human support, and make available to them the means and opportunities that will enable them to continue to carry out their leading role in the armed revolution, until they liberate their homeland.

Article 16: The liberation of Palestine, from a spiritual point of view, will provide the Holy Land with an atmosphere of safety and tranquility, which in turn will safeguard the country's religious sanctuaries and guarantee freedom of worship and of visit to all, without discrimination of race, color, language, or religion. Accordingly, the people of Palestine look to all spiritual forces in the world for support.

Article 19: The partition of Palestine in 1947 and the establishment of the state of Israel are entirely illegal, regardless of the passage of time, because they were contrary to the will of the Palestinian people and to their natural right in their homeland, and inconsistent with the principles embodied in the Charter of the United Nations, particularly the right to self-determination.

Article 20: The Balfour Declaration, the Mandate for Palestine, and everything that has been based upon them, are deemed null and void. Claims of historical or religious ties of Jews with Palestine are incompatible with the facts of history and the true conception of what constitutes statehood. *Judaism, being a religion, is not an independent nationality. Nor do Jews constitute a single nation with an identity of its own; they are citizens of the states to which they belong.*

Article 23: *The demand of security and peace, as well as the demand of right and justice, require all states to consider Zionism an illegitimate movement, to outlaw its existence, and to ban its operations, in order that friendly relations among peoples may be preserved, and the loyalty of citizens to their respective homelands safeguarded.*

Article 24: *The Palestinian people believe in the principles of justice, freedom, sovereignty, self-determination, human dignity, and in the right of all peoples to exercise them.*

Article 30: *Fighters and carriers of arms in the war of liberation are the nucleus of the popular army, which will be the protective force for the gains of the Palestinian Arab people.*

Fatah

Fatah, under the current leadership of Mahmoud Abbas, is an outgrowth of the Palestinian Liberation Organization. Abbas is being classified as a moderate and is the Palestinian "peace partner" with whom Israel is now attempting to negotiate (with the very strong encouragement of the U.S. government).

Fatah is also known as the Palestine Liberation Organization (PLO). The Movement for the National Liberation of Palestine (Fatah) was founded in the early 1960s by the late Yasser Arafat and friends of his in Algeria. Fatah was originally opposed to the founding of the PLO, which it viewed as a political rival. Backed by Syria, Fatah began carrying out terrorist raids against Israeli targets in 1965, launched from Jordan, Lebanon, and Egyptian-occupied Gaza. Dozens of raids were carried out each year, exclusively against civilian targets.

Fatah's popularity among Palestinians grew until it took over control of the PLO in 1968.

The word Fatah means "conquest, victory, triumph" in Arabic.

In December 2007, Palestinian Authority chairman Mahmoud Abbas told reporters: "Historically there are two states, Israel and Palestine. Israel is inhabited by Jews and others. We are willing to recognize that and nothing else." Saturday, December 1, 2007, (IsraelNN.com)

Al–Qaeda

Also known as the International Front for Fighting Jews and Crusaders; Islamic Army; Islamic Army for the Liberation of Holy Sites; Islamic Salvation Foundation; The Base; The Group for the Preservation of the Holy Sites; The Islamic Army for the Liberation of the Holy Places; The World Islamic Front for Jihad Against Jews and Crusaders; Usama bin Ladin Network; Osama bin Laden Organization

"Al-Qaeda" is Arabic for "the base."

Al-Qaeda is an international terrorist network led by Osama bin Laden. Established in 1988 by bin Laden, al-Qaeda helped finance, recruit, transport, and train thousands of fighters from dozens of countries to be part of the Afghan resistance to defeat the Soviet Union. To continue the Holy War beyond Afghanistan, al-Qaeda's current goal is to establish a pan-Islamic Caliphate throughout the world by working with allied Islamic extremist groups to overthrow regimes it deems "non-Islamic" and to expel Westerners and non-Muslims from Muslim countries.

In February 1998, al-Qaeda issued a statement under the banner of "The World Islamic Front for Jihad Against the Jews and Crusaders," stating it was the duty of all Muslims to kill "US citizens, civilian or military" and their allies everywhere. Al-Qaeda would merge with Egyptian Islamic Jihad (Al-Jihad) of Ayman al-Zawahiri in June 2001.

After al-Qaeda's September 11, 2001, attacks on America, the United States launched a war in Afghanistan to destroy al-Qaeda's bases there and overthrow the Taliban, the country's Muslim fundamentalist rulers who harbored bin Laden and his followers.

Hezbollah

Also known as the Party of God; Islamic Jihad; Islamic Jihad for the Liberation of Palestine.

Hezbollah is a Lebanese organization of several thousand Shiite militants that opposes the West and Israel and seeks to create in Lebanon a Muslim fundamentalist state modeled on Iran. Its primary mission is to destroy the state of Israel and, in the process, to murder as many Jews as possible. Describing itself as "an Islamic struggle movement," Hezbollah condemns "the Zionist occupation of Palestine" and candidly states that it "sees no legitimacy for the existence of Israel."

Hezbollah means "Party of God."

The Hezbollah founding statement contains a section entitled, "The Necessity for the Destruction of Israel," which reads: "We see in Israel the vanguard of the United States in our Islamic world. It is the hated enemy that must be fought until the hated ones get what they deserve. Our primary assumption in our fight against Israel states that the Zionist entity is aggressive from its inception, and built on lands wrested from their owners, at the expense of the rights of the Muslim people. Therefore our struggle will end only when this entity is obliterated. We recognize no treaty with it, no cease-fire, and no peace agreements, whether separate or consolidated. We vigorously condemn all plans for negotiation with Israel, and regard all negotiators as enemies, for the reason that such negotiation is nothing but the recognition of the legitimacy of the Zionist occupation of Palestine."

Hezbollah and its affiliates have planned or been linked to a lengthy series of terrorist attacks against the United States, Israel, and other Western targets. These attacks include:[7]

- a series of kidnappings of Westerners in Lebanon, including several Americans in the 1980s;

- suicide truck bombings that killed more than 200 U.S. Marines at their barracks in Beirut, Lebanon, in 1983;

- the 1985 hijacking of TWA flight 847, which featured the famous footage of the plane's pilot leaning out of the cockpit with a gun to his head;

- two major attacks in the 1990s on Jewish targets in

---

[7] Council on Foreign Relations, http://www.cfr.org/publication/9155/

Argentina. The 1992 bombing of the Israeli Embassy that claimed twenty-nine victims and the 1994 bombing of a Jewish community center where ninety-five people were killed;

- a July, 2006, raid on a border post in northern Israel in which two Israeli soldiers were taken captive. The abductions sparked an Israeli military campaign against Lebanon, to which Hezbollah responded by firing rockets across the Lebanese border into Israel.

Mahmoud Ahmadinejad Comes to the United States

The phone call came as I was forming matzo balls for a dear friend's "Jewish penicillin" – the delicious chicken broth soup with ping-pong-ball-sized matzo balls (dumplings). Her chemotherapy had caused some severe complications, and the request for a to-go order had been phoned in to me from her daughter earlier that day.

"This is Victor," I answered, my phone cradled between my ear and shoulder with the gooey matzo mixture cupped in my palms.

On the other end of the phone was David Brog who announced more than asked, "Victor, you are aware of President Ahmadinejad's upcoming visit to the United Nations in a couple of days? The Conference of Presidents of Major American Jewish Organizations has asked Pastor Hagee to speak at the protest rally."

"That's awesome!" I cheered into the phone.

David continued, "Pastor's schedule is such that he just can't be there and we would like you to go on his behalf."

"Huh?!?" I understandably answered. (This scenario caused me to imagine an important occasion where an organization like NASA has been asked to send a world-renowned astronaut to make a presentation. The astronaut is unable to attend the event. NASA goes into their laboratory and grabs a monkey [who was simply a part of an experiment in space, but did in fact fly in a shuttle] and sends him in the astronaut's place!)

With much reassurance from my wife, friends, and CUFI leaders, three days later I grabbed a banana and caught an 8-hour flight to the East Coast.

My entire time in New York was like a dream. While backstage outside the United Nations building with the other speakers waiting to be introduced to the crowd of over 25,000 protestors (and surrounded by New York's finest dressed in full riot gear, including some monster-lookin' machine guns) I observed a parade of attractive young people passing by. I won't ever allow myself to forget the moment..

A long line of Israeli teenagers briskly walked through a small but shrill anti-Israel protest, and then passed directly in front of me.

Curly, jet-black-haired schoolgirls holding hands and chattering in Hebrew alongside handsome, ruddy-faced Jewish young men with dark brown eyes, set straight ahead, together marching purposely to join their swarming family of thousands in front of the staging area.

As I smiled, and considered their determined strength and beauty, I heard the voice of history: "Just 65 years ago, millions of these young men and women marched into mass graves their brothers and sisters were forced to dig. Today they are being forced to remember, and forced to find an answer for why President Ahmadinejad has been allowed to come into their world, mock them, and mock the remembrance of their sorrow. These young Jews are also being forced to wonder if 'Never Again' is just a delusion."

As I stepped up to the podium and glanced out at the rolling landscape of pro-Israel supporters, I spoke with the weight of this history pressing upon my heart.

At the conclusion of my speech, (see below) I had the immense privilege of offering Ahmadinejad the thoughts of millions of Americans as together we shouted, "*Yi'mach Sh'mo!*" (Hebrew equivalent of "go to hell!")

In the Words of the Torah:

"*The offering of the wicked is exceedingly disgusting and abhorrent to the Lord*" (Proverbs 21:27). *How much more when he brings it with evil intention.*

Ahmadinejad! Take heed when you mock the sacred ground of this city where the Twin Towers stood. The stench of your hypocritical wreath offering is an abomination to the Almighty, and it is to us.

Mahmoud Ahmadinejad! Yi'mach Sh'mo! Yi'mach Sh'mo! Yi'mach Sh'mo!

For my Christian readers:

Yi'mach Sh'mo is Hebrew for "may his name be blotted out forever." Every year when the Book of Esther is read during Purim, all the Jewish children shout this phrase every time there is a mention of the wicked Haman.

I fear for my children and grandchildren.

The world's leaders have lost their way.

Why was this man not arrested on the spot for incitement to genocide?

The majority of people who listened to Ahmadinejad's opening prayers the following day at the United Nations and his speech at Columbia University during his September 2007, U.S. visit had absolutely no concept of what they were hearing.

In 2006 Ahmadinejad offered a similar prayer during his opening remarks when he addressed the United Nations:

> "In the name of God, the Compassionate, the Merciful. Praise be to God and peace be upon Prophet Mohammad and His Infallible Household and chosen disciples. O God, hasten the reappearance of the Imam of the times and grant to us victory and prosperity. Include us among his followers and martyrs."

Include us among his followers and martyrs?

He's kidding, right?

The 12th Imam

To understand the horror of Ahmadinejad's supplication, you must understand the meaning within the theology of his religion. Ahmadinejad, along with many other Shiite Muslims, awaits the coming of the 12th Shiite Imam, Muhammed ibn Hasan. They consider him to be the last direct male descendent of the Prophet Mohammed's son-in-law Aliâ, who disappeared in 874 AD.

Ahmadinejad's particular brand of Shiism holds that this 12th Imam, also called the Mahdi, (meaning "Ruler of Time") is living at the bottom of a well in Jankaran, Iran.

Followers of this belief drop written prayers into the well to petition him.

Waiting for the rapture in Iran

By Scott Peterson | Staff writer of The Christian Science Monitor

December 21, 2005 edition

JAMKARAN, IRAN: "For those who believe, the devotion is real. Tears stream down the cheeks of 2,000 men ripe for the return of the Mahdi, the 12th Imam they expect will soon emerge to bring justice and peace to a corrupt world. Eyes stare upward and arms open wide to receive God's promised salvation. The storyteller's lyrical song speaks of tragedy on the path to salvation, prompting cries of anguish and joy. As at a Christian revivalist meeting that promises healing and redemption, many weep as they pray for the Shiite Muslim version of the second coming of the Messiah.

"All Muslims believe in a coming Mahdi as a messianic figure who will destroy the enemies of Islam. Islamic tradition pictures the Mahdi as joining with the army of Muslim warriors carrying black flags. The Mahdi will then lead this army to Israel and re-conquer it for Islam. The Jews will be slaughtered until very few remain and Jerusalem will become the location of the Mahdi's rule over the Earth where all infidels (non-Muslims) convert to Islam and live according to 'Sharia.'"[8]

These events occur prior to a second physical coming of Hadhrat Isa bin Maryam (Jesus, son of Mary), whom Islam believes was a prophet of God from the lineage of Abraham, and will accompany the Mahdi upon his return.

The Quran has several accounts concerning Jesus that are similar to those in the New Testament.

> *From the Quran Chapter 19:*
>
> *Relate in the Book the story of Mary, when she withdrew from her family to a place in the East. She placed a screen to screen herself from them; then we sent her our angel, and he appeared before her as a man in all respects.*
>
> *She said: "I seek refuge from you to God Most Gracious: come not near if you do fear God."*
>
> *He said: "Nay, I am only a messenger from your Lord, to announce to you the gift of a Holy son."*
>
> *She said: "How will I have a son, seeing that no man has touched me, and I am not unchaste."*
>
> *He said: "So it will be: Your Lord says, 'That is easy for Me: And We wish to appoint him as a Sign unto men and a Mercy from Us.' It is a matter so decreed."... Such was Jesus, the Son of Mary: it is a statement of truth, about which they vainly dispute.*

Shiite Islamic scholars believe Jesus is coming back to earth soon, to serve as a deputy to the Mahdi who will destroy the infidels.

From the Islamic book *Tazkarat ol-Olia*: "the Mahdi will come with Jesus son of Mary accompanying him," the series explains. "This indicates that these two great men are to complement each other. Imam

---

[8] Sharia is the system of civil law that is based upon the Quran and the Ahadith (the oral record of the sayings of Mohammad) and the work of Muslim scholars in the first two centuries of Islam. Sharia is a code for living to which Muslims should adhere, including prayers, fasting, and donations to the poor. It is interpreted in many different ways throughout the many different expressions of the Muslim faith.

Mahdi will be the leader while Prophet Jesus will act as his lieutenant in the struggle against oppression and establishment of justice in the world."

These events are said to happen before all Muslim believers die, and prior to the Day of Judgment, during which a resurrection of the dead, involving judgment and punishment, occurs. It is after this that Allah establishes his kingdom on Earth, with Islam as the worldwide religion.

Ahmadinejad's Apocalyptic Politics

Ahmadinejad's Shiism teaches that "chaos and bloodshed" must usher in the coming of the 12th Imam. Unlike the Christian (and Orthodox Jewish) theology, which teaches Messiah will come preceded by waves of immorality, wars, and divinely decreed natural disasters, the chaos that summons the Mahdi is wholly the responsibility of human action. Therefore, the one chosen to bring about the conditions that will free Mahdi to come and free mankind would be an eternally revered figure indeed.

> ### From: MEMRI (Middle East Media Research Institute):
>
> In his recently published memoirs, French Foreign Minister Philippe Douste-Blazy relates the story of a meeting between three European foreign ministers together with Javier Solana of the European Union and Iranian President Mahmoud Ahmadinejad. The meeting, which took place at the United Nations on September 15 2005, dealt with what Douste-Blazy characterized as "the generous European offer" to Iran regarding its nuclear program. Ahmadinejad was characterized by Douste-Blazy, a surgeon and a professor of medicine by profession, as stubborn, and the meeting was described as leading nowhere.
>
> Suddenly, Ahmadinejad changed the course of the conversation with the following aside: "Do you know why we should wish to have chaos at any price?" he asked

rhetorically. "Because, after the chaos, we can see the greatness of Allah."

Ahmadinejad has made it clear by the use of his political power that he is a true believer in this Shiite end of days theology. When he previously served as Mayor of Tehran, he promoted a building project to widen the roads to accommodate the Mahdi's triumphal entry into the city. One of his first acts of office as President of Iran was to dedicate approximately $20 million to the restoration and improvement of the mosque at Jamkaran, near the well where the Mahdi is claimed to dwell.

Ahmadinejad's Apocalyptic Destiny

The apocalyptic scenario of Ahmadinejad's faith combined with Iran's nuclear ambitions must be understood as being intrinsically linked. When he insists that Iran's nuclear development program is a peaceful one, he really means it. The great "chaos and bloodshed" ushering in the return of the 12th Imam and a new dawn of Islamic worldwide dominance is Ahmadinejad's peace plan. Ahmadinejad believes he has been chosen to create the cataclysmic events that will beckon the promised Mahdi to return. He defines his nuclear ambition as peaceful since it would give him the power to "wipe Israel off the map," and bring about a nuclear response against Iran that would surely follow.

In Ahmadinejad's aberrant and hate-filled theology, this is how peace shall come upon the earth: nuclear chaos will bring the return of Mahdi, the Muslimization of the world, and finally, Sharia law.

The belief in his personal divine importance was best confirmed after his U.N. speech in September 2008, which was laden with references to the Mahdi. Upon his return to Iran he met with Ayatollah Javadi-Amoli, where the two discussed an alleged paranormal occurrence while Ahmadinejad spoke. He related to the cleric:

> *On the last day when I was speaking, one of our group told me that when I started to say, "Bismillah (with the blessings of) Muhammad," he saw a green light come from*

around me, and I was placed inside this aura. I felt it myself. I felt that the atmosphere suddenly changed, and for those 27 or 28 minutes, all the leaders of the world did not blink. When I say they didn't move an eyelid, I'm not exaggerating.

They were looking as if a hand was holding them there, and had just opened their eyes. "Alhamdulillah!" (Praise to Allah)

Mahmoud Ahmadinejad. Excerpted from *The Mystical Menace of Mahmoud Ahmadinejad* by Daniel Pipes, New York Sun, January 10, 2006.

Another portion of Shiite belief is built around a culture of martyrdom. The Shiia assumes persecution against true Islamic believers will come because of the infidels' hatred of their righteous conduct. Consider Ahmadinejad's speech given to a gathering of families of martyrs in 2006:

We are all obliged to keep alive the culture of martyrdom-seeking in the society. Culture of martyrdom-seeking is our most effective weapon and best guarantee for our national security. Ruthless enemies who have a chronic enmity against our country and our nation have not succeeded in achieving their objectives so far thanks to the existence of this culture of martyrdom-seeking among our nation.

He who is ready for martyrdom is always victorious. Martyrdom is the peak of mankind's perfection and the martyrs enjoy the highest status of humanity in this world and the Hereafter. People spend tough years of strenuous work in a bid to achieve the peaks of grandeur and pride, while our dear martyrs achieved those high peaks in shortest possible time.

Non-Negotiables of Faith

The leaders of our nation must wake up to the religious ideology driving the political agenda of Ahmadinejad and other militant Muslim groups around the world. The use of martyrdom and weapons of mass destruction are not only entirely appropriate in the minds of these devoted followers of their faith,they are divinely sanctioned and "holy" justified.

Hoping religiously motivated zealots can be forced into becoming moderates by talk or sanction is to not understand them at all. Their holy war against all infidels is central to their Islamic ideology. It is a non-negotiable pillar of their faith.

My Torah-loving Jewish friends will never switch "Shabbat" to Wednesday, or Thursday, or any other day. It is an eternal portion of the Jewish faith. God commanded to keep the Sabbath starting every Friday at sundown, and if you are an observant Jew, Shabbat is Shabbat and that's that. It is a non-negotiable facet of their faith.

For my Christian readers:

Shabbat is Hebrew for Sabbath. Most Jews spend Friday evening holding a Shabbat family dinner where they pray, sing, and bless wives and children.

Exodus 20:8 "Remember the Sabbath day by keeping it holy."

The day of rest ends on Saturday evening at sundown.

Christianity's first-century adaptation of Sunday as our day of rest was partially motivated by early anti-Semitism. The Sabbath was re-interpreted by the church in Rome to be a temporary institution given to the Jews as a sign of their unfaithfulness. Christians were encouraged to show their disassociation from the Jewish Sabbath by fasting on that day, by abstaining from the Lord's Supper, and by not attending religious assemblies.

Samuele Bacchiocchi, PhD, Andrews University

Though some suggest that Jesus was simply unconscious when taken from the cross and placed in the tomb, Christians believe He died and was resurrected from the dead. We are unable to change our doctrine of belief into something more rational.

It is a non-negotiable facet of the Christian faith.

We must understand there is no negotiating position acceptable to the supporters of the militant Muslim faith apart from the complete and unconditional submission of the non-Muslim world to the rule of Sharia. Our nation's leaders must comprehend and accept diplomacy's absolute impotence when battling against such religious fanaticism.

As the nation of Israel celebrated its 60th anniversary, Iranian President Mahmoud Ahmadinejad branded the Jewish state as a "stinking corpse that was doomed to disappear." Shortly after his statement and during the U.S. presidential debates, two candidates were asked, "If you are the President of the United States and Iran attacks Israel with nuclear weapons what would be your response?"

The first candidate answered, "The United States would respond with nuclear weapons against Iran."

The second candidate stated, "We would respond with nuclear weapons and we could obliterate Iran."

I felt physically sick upon hearing and considering their answers.

There is an obvious and ominous problem with the way these candidates answered the question concerning Iran attacking Israel with nuclear weapons.

If Iran has attacked Israel with nuclear weapons, it is too late.

- There is no more Israel.

- 5.5 million Jews are dead.

- 1.2 million Arabs living in Israel are dead and if the United States obliterates Iran, 70 million Iranians will be dead.

"The only rational answer to the question of Iran attacking Israel with nuclear weapons is for every world leader to say, 'I assure Israel and the world that Iran will never possess a nuclear weapon.'"

Our nation was once committed to this promise but our leaders in Washington are losing their resolve. Today, Iran has moved one day closer to possessing nuclear capabilities and wiping Israel off the map, as the nation has repeatedly promised to accomplish.

Loving Our Enemies

I am familiar with the New Testament teaching of Jesus exhorting us to "love our enemies" and "bless those who persecute us." As a Christian, I believe I am the recipient of God's loving kindness extended to me while I was His enemy.

From this unmerited and merciful love, we have created the abbreviated sound-bite Christian theology of "love the sinner, but hate the sin."

The slogan makes a great bumper sticker and has a nice sound to it and the worse the crime, the nobler we appear when suggesting "turning the other cheek" and loving an enemy of heinous enormity.

But such response is hardly suitable when a monster has blown our own child to shreds, tortured and decapitated our husband, or raped and murdered our wife. When answering the unimaginable pain of another whose life has been ravished with such darkness, our offering that "we must love the sinner, but hate the sin" would be a callous comfort.

There are New Testament examples of Jesus exhibiting abhorrence toward sin and sinners.

John 2:13-16:

When it was almost time for the Jewish Passover, Jesus went up to Jerusalem. In the temple courts he found men selling cattle, sheep and doves, and others sitting at tables exchanging money. So he made a whip out of cords, and drove all from the temple area, both sheep and cattle; he scattered the coins of the moneychangers and overturned their tables. To those who sold doves he said, "Get these out of here! How dare you turn my Father's house into a market!"

Luke 17:1-2:

Jesus said to His disciples, "It is inevitable that stumbling

blocks come, but woe to him through whom they come! It
would be better for him if a millstone was hung around his
neck and he was thrown into the sea, than that he would
cause one of these little ones to stumble."

Come on now.

The best thing to do with anyone who would damage the lives of
little ones is to drown them? I know it is a Hebraism, but if you simply
cannot bring yourself to admit that Jesus abhors certain enemies of his
people, then at least be honest with the implications of this scripture.
Jesus not only hates this type of sin, but He also has a very, very, very
strong dislike toward the unrepentant folks that perpetrate it.

Romans 12:9:

Love must be sincere. *Hate what is evil; cling to what is*
good.

You can categorize these scriptures however you want, but you
can't call them love nor even tough love.

I am not suggesting that harboring hatred is ever a Christian
alternative to forgiveness.

A root of bitterness toward anyone who has sinned against you
will eventually devour you from the inside out. Refusing to forgive
someone and hoping for their demise is like drinking poison – and
hoping they die. There are times when forgiving simply means releasing
our demands for vengeance and committing the guilty party into the
hands of God and His judgments. Volumes of books have been written
on this theme.

Forgiveness: The Power and the Puzzles by Wendell E. Miller,
Clearbrook Publishers, August 1994, is one of the best I've ever read.

Answering the Question:
"You love your enemies? How can you love the terrorists that are killing our children in Israel?"

The wearisome "we must hate the sin...love the sinner" is just one of the shallow answers given to difficult and painful questions asked by the Jewish community. We Christians tend to preach a theological high road to others, especially when confronted with scenarios that do not touch our lives in a personal way.

I conclude with what I believe to be a Biblically accurate and compassionate answer to the specific question of loving the suicidal, militant Islamic terrorists whose goals include the destruction of the nation of Israel.

Answer: Followers of the New Testament are instructed to love our enemies. We are also taught, "Our love must be sincere and we must abhor evil." I abhor the wicked ideology and actions of the militant Islamic movement. When the last deed of a person's life is a suicide attack upon innocent men, women, and children, I believe God abhors both the act and the person committing it and so do I.

Psalm 11:5:

The Lord tests the righteous and the wicked, and the one who loves violence His soul hates.

Proverbs 6:16-19:

There are six things the Lord hates, seven that are detestable to him: haughty eyes, a lying tongue, hands that shed innocent blood, a heart that devises wicked schemes, feet that are quick to rush into evil, a false witness who pours out lies and a man who stirs up dissension among brothers.

Question 9

"What would you say if a Jew told you he wanted to convert to Christianity?"

Standard Christian Answer:
"Praise the Lord!"

I had been flown out to New York University to give a lecture to a room full of Jewish college students.

The one Christian student in attendance did not approve of my answer to her question and had literally just stormed out of the hall, slamming the door behind her.

"Don't worry, she's one of mine," I grimaced, attempting to negate the awkwardness of the moment. (She was actually a Christian anti-Semite and I had inadvertently exposed her darkened way of thinking to her dismay, disagreement, and apparent great disapproval.)

These college kids had been tough on me. The atmosphere had the intensity of a physics final as I began my presentation. My "always-work laugh lines" had barely produced a single turn of the lips from the mass of emotionless and large-brained young faces staring at me.

I began to realize this was probably the first time most of the attendees had ever been face to face with a real live evangelical pastor.

"What do you think about religious mixed marriages?" a young man wanted to know, with a slight sarcastic tone seasoning his question.

"The Torah prohibits Jews marrying outside of the Jewish faith, as does the New Testament in regard to Christians marrying non-Christian. My wife and I do a lot of premarital counseling, and in the case of mixed religious couples I just can't perform the wedding ceremony," I honestly answered.

The atmosphere in the room changed from understandingly apprehensive to uncomfortably silent.

"How can I ask God to bless something the Scriptures teach is not a blessing?" I rhetorically asked, attempting to clarify my theological dilemma.

My response lit a grass fire of hissing debate that blew through the lecture hall.

"Listen, I'm not the 'czar of marriage' or anything, and people can go to the County Court House and get married to anyone they want, and of course I'll support their marriage!" I loudly and sincerely protested so as not to appear to be the religious jerk I suddenly felt like.

"I just personally feel I can't officiate at a wedding ceremony with mixed..."

"What would you do if a Jew told you he wanted to convert to Christianity?" another student shouted out, cutting short my answer and immediately ending the whispering clamor in the lecture hall.

I paused for a moment to enjoy the calm and answered with a smile of relief, "I'd send him away three times, my friend."

For my Christian readers:

Jews don't seek out converts. There is an age-old tradition of turning down a potential convert three times, which possibly comes from the Middle Ages, when a convert and the converter would be killed. Due to the arduous path of conversion, the tradition continues in order to discourage those who are not truly sincere in their spiritual interest of Judaism.

"Well, what would you do if a Christian told you he was converting to Judaism?" the same young man followed up, now smiling.

"He'd still be in the family – I wouldn't have a problem with it" I quipped.

Finally a little laughter echoed through the hall.

I then answered with absolute seriousness, "Listen, what a person chooses to believe concerning God is what they believe. That's why it's called faith."

From Rock & Roll to the Rock of My Salvation

I recently came across a letter I had written almost forty years ago.

Having just graduated from high school, I wrote this letter to my parents. I listed the "10 Reasons I Want To Be A Musician" in an attempt to explain my dire need to drop out of junior college and join a band with a guy named Eddie who had just quit a band with a national hit single called, "Hey Momma, Keep Yo' Big Mouth Shut." My parents should have seen it coming.

I received my first guitar when I was four years old, began guitar lessons when I was seven, started my first band in the 6th grade, and worked as a guitar instructor at a music studio at age fifteen. It was so obviously my destiny to be a rock star but somehow my parents had not yet completely noticed.

Here are a few of my deep thoughts concerning my life at seventeen years old. I can't remember why I wrote in all caps or why I didn't proofread this significant document before handing it to my parents.

- I WOULD LIKE TO BE A PROFESSIONAL MUSICIAN.

- I WANT TO TRAVEL AND PLAY IN CLUBS.

- I WOULD MORE ABOUT MUSIC THAT I COULD APPLY TO MY PLAYING THAN I AM PRESENTLY LEARNING AT SCHOOL.

- ALTHOUGH I ENJOY GOING TO SCHOOL, I HAVE NO INSENTIVE TO STUDY BECAUSE THE MATERIAL I MUST STUDY IS SIMPLY MEMORIZED FOR A TEST, AND THEN FORGOTTEN WEEKS LATER BECAUSE IT IS NEVER APPLYED TO ANYTHING IN MY INTERESTS.

- EDDIE HAS ALOT OF CONNECTIONS AND HE KNOWS

MANY PEOPLE WHO CAN HELP US SUCCED WITH OUR MUSIC.

- EVEN IF THE GROUP BREAKS UP AND I HAVE TO START ALL OVER AGAIN, AT LEAST I WILL BE DOING SOMETHING THAT I WANT TO DO, AND THAT'S WHAT LIFE IS ALL ABOUT.

I remember writing this and reading it over and over again thinking, "Man, maybe I should be an attorney!" It just seemed so convincing at the time.

Just like my belief that I would have a ponytail forever.

I left college and recorded some songs with Eddie. We were sure we had another national hit single on our hands with 'Stop That Train,'

a heavy metal rocker with a great chorus:

"Stop that train – Stop that train – Stop that train, from movin' – my baby's inside!"

While headlining with Eddie's new band at Yuba City's lavish Kabuki Lounge and Bowling Alley, I was busted for being under twenty-one by the ABC cops (Alcohol Beverage Control). I took it as a sign from the gods of rock and left Eddie to go back and rejoin a band with a bunch of my former high school friends.

We all decided to quit our day jobs and move in together.

It was 1972 and I was now part of a rock & roll commune, living on an old abandoned 140-acre dairy farm with ten of my best friends, traveling around the country playing concerts and beer bars. We had a large organic garden, horses, goats, ducks, cats, lots of dogs, and lots of everything, except money.

Our hair got really long and our band got really good and we were living the "Age of Aquarius" dream.

There were many young people of our generation who were still looking for their dream. There were many looking for truth, or looking to "find themselves." Some were even looking for God.

I was not a part of any of these groups. I was a professional hippy and only looking for whoever was having a party that night.

Truth...religion...church...God...Christianity??

I assure you, none of these things were even remotely on my list of "things to do before I die."

One of our band managers was a member of the Baha'i faith. Though he would often pontificate about spirituality, his life example was so dubious that even within our purple hazy worldview, the "truth" he was peddling found no buyers amongst us.

Jesus Freaks would often accost us as we traveled across the country.

When an eighty-passenger school bus pulls into your little city and eleven people, all with hair down to their elbows, stumble into your local hamburger stand, you got trouble and if you're a Jesus Freak you got a mission 'cause you literally got a bus load of sinners in town.

Jesus Freaks!

We seemed to be prime targets for the young men and women of our generation who had "found Jesus" and loved telling others about Him (whether they wanted to hear it or not).

Some of the passionate preachers of "the way" left us with the very clear impression that our lives were definitely happier and possibly saner than theirs. Others would say little, but leave us with unsolicited Bibles or Jesus Tracts.

Every now and then we would cross paths with common, yet extraordinary New Testament believers who would possess a near irresistible fragrance of hope in the simple story they would tell of God's eternal and sacrificial love for us.

I resisted it all.

My rock 'n' roll dream life had long lost its glimmer, and even though I went to bed and woke every morning agonizingly bored with the meaningless of my life, I detested and despised the very thought of ever becoming a religious nut.

Though God was most definitely not on my list, apparently I was on His.

On November 10, 1973, during a tour with our band in Ashland, Oregon, I woke up in a hotel room and, feeling the familiar and dreaded weight of my empty life, I prayed to Jesus for the first time as an adult. Opening the nightstand drawer, I pulled out a Gideon's Bible and began reading from the Book of Isaiah. About a month later I had almost finished reading the entire Bible and had concluded a couple of things.

First of all, I believed that Jesus died for my sins. Secondly, I realized if I was going to try and hang out with Him and His Father, I really needed to change some of my ways or I was probably going to be in big trouble.

I called a band meeting and announced to my band mates, "I think I'm a Christian now and there are a few things I'm pretty sure I shouldn't be doing anymore."

My friends rolled their eyes, moaned and giggled, and told me I was going to be all right.

One year later, as we began our last concert tour together, each member of the band had come to a faith in Christ.

Thirty-five Years Later

Over thirty-five years later a number of us still eat dinner together every Friday night. We usually light a few candles, thank the Lord for our families, sing from the Psalms, pray for our children (and grandchildren!), and pray for one another.

We also pray for the peace of Jerusalem and blessing upon the Jewish people.

None of us are Jewish; we are "goyim" through and through. We jokingly refer to our Friday night Shabbat gatherings as our "goy-bat" celebration. But we, like millions of evangelical Christians across the nation have been taught from the Scriptures: Though God loves everybody, He loved the Jews first.

We believe the Jews are a very unique and very precious people in the heart of God.

Christian Conversion

We have a saying, "Going to McDonalds doesn't make you a hamburger and going to church doesn't make you a Christian."

I share my conversion story so as to clarify what the experience means in evangelical Christian vernacular. The only steps to becoming a Christian within Protestant theology are within the heart of the one seeking out the claims of Jesus Christ. The act of personally trusting in His death and resurrection as being the means of acquiring righteousness before God, is the Christian definition of being "born again."

Evangelicals identify with the pardon of God through faith in Christ, in similarity to the crediting of righteousness by faith granted to Abram in the Book of Genesis.

Genesis 15:5-6:

And He took him outside, and said "Gaze, now toward the Heavens, and count the stars if you are able to count them!" And He said to him, "So shall your offspring be!" And he trusted in HaShem, and He reckoned it to him as righteousness.

Ephesians 2:8-9:

For by grace you have been saved through faith; and that not of yourselves, it is the gift of God; not as a result of works, so that no one may boast.

Coming to believe God personally knows and loves you can be a bit life changing to a rock & roll hippy or to anyone for that matter. Telling others about your life-changing discovery is hard not to do.

The Jesus Freaks who often *harshed our mello* (irked us) in their sharing the "good news" during our hippy days, were simply telling us their life-changing "B.C. to A.D." story. It didn't always sound like good news to us, but that generally depended on the maturity and motivation of the messengers.

I quote from David Brog's book, *Standing With Israel:*

While most Jews are aware of the centuries of pain caused by Christian efforts to convert them, few evangelicals are as well versed in their Jewish history. For evangelicals, sharing the gospel comes as naturally as sharing a hidden treasure: they have found something that has brought them great joy, and with the best of intentions they want to pass it on. What Jews call proselytizing, evangelicals earnestly call "sharing the good news." Most evangelicals cannot imagine that someone would take offense at such a gesture. Sensitivity here, as in so many instances, must be taught. And the teachers, the ones sharing the Jewish perspective with the evangelical grassroots, are typically those who have come to understand these concerns through their close collaboration with the Jews.

In the blessing and cauldron of our two faiths being drawn together, genuine relationships are being forged. Within many of these new relations, I believe true Christian love and respect are replacing historic Christian hatred and perversity. Christians and Jews are becoming friends and as in all intimate friendships, the shallow, old, dusty taboos of discussing politics and religion are swept away.

One such friendship I have is with Fred Hayward.

Every time we sit down together we talk like a couple of fifteen-year-old girls on Red Bull. And because we talk, we talk a lot about everything that is important to us. We talk about every facet of our lives.

The fact that I am a Christian makes faith one of the central portions of my life, and there are times when we discuss the Christian faith. The fact that Fred is a Jew, makes all things Jewish a central part of his life, and there are times when we discuss the Jewish faith.

Fred has heard the "good news" from me – not because of a belief on my part that I can convert him, but as an outgrowth of our genuine friendship.

I am deeply touched and delighted in how he sums up the receiving end of his friendship with Christians. In an e-mail responding to the New York Times concerning a Christian Zionist article they published, Fred writes:

> I am a Jew who has gotten to know (and love) several of Pastor Hagee's followers in Christians United for Israel. They have never once tried to convert me in preparation for "The Rapture." It is simply not part of their theology.
>
> Indeed, their unconditional honoring of my heritage has led me to be more 'Jewish.' And, they have never failed to be there for me, always without asking, whenever they thought I might need some help.
>
> Fred Hayward
>
> Sacramento, CA.

The Jew's "Good News"

Although it is possible for a gentile to convert into the Jewish faith, it is not necessary in Jewish theology for gentiles to do so to be deemed "righteous" before God.

The Jews preach a "good news" message to the gentiles called the Seven Noahide Laws. Most of my Torah-loving Jewish friends bring it up early (and often) in our relationship as they believe it is God's commanded way for non-Jews to "merit a share in the World to Come," the Jewish equivalence of heaven.

They share their convictions with me, concerning my eternal future because of their concern and love for me.

For my Christian readers:

"Anyone who accepts upon himself the fulfillment of these Seven Mitzvos [commandments] and is precise in their observance is considered one of the *Hasidei Umot Ha'olam* (Righteous of the nations of the world) and will merit a share in the world to come."

From the classic commentary by the Rambam, Rav Moshe ben Maimon (Maimonides), in *The Laws of Kings* 8:11.

The Seven Noahide Laws

1. Do not murder.
2. Do not steal.
3. Do not worship false gods.
4. Do not be sexually immoral.
5. Do not eat a limb from a live animal.
6. Do not curse God.
7. Do set up courts and bring offenders to justice.

I am honored to spend an hour each week, learning with Sacramento Chabad Director, Rabbi Mendy Cohen. I told him I was pleased to report I found myself to be reasonably observant of the Noahide Laws – and absolutely aghast at the very thought of one of them in particular.

"Rabbi, who in the world would eat a limb from a living animal?" I squeamishly groaned.

"A hungry hunter," he taught me, smiling.

For my Christian readers:

Chabad-Lubavitch (also known as Chabad, Habad or Lubavitch), is one of the largest branches of Hasidic Judaism and one of the largest Jewish movements worldwide, especially in the United States, the Former Soviet Union, Europe and Israel. Chabad is a Hebrew acronym for "*Chochmah*, Binah, *Da'at*" ("Wisdom, Understanding, Knowledge").[9] Lubavitch, taken from the Russian Lyubavichi, is the name of the town that served as the movement's headquarters for over a century. In 1993 there were over 200,000 adherents to the movement.[10,11,12] Some estimate today that there are over a million.[13]

Jewish tradition teaches that God first gave six of these seven laws to Adam in the garden of Eden, presented them to all humanity through Noah, (including the seventh law pertaining to eating meat), and reiterated them within the Oral Torah at Mt. Sinai to the children of Israel. The precise observance of these seven commandments required for a gentile to find his way into the Hebrew world to come actually demands the acceptance of many more observances within the Jewish tradition of all that these laws encompass.

---

[9] About Chabad-Lubavitch on Chabad.org

[10] Wertheimer, Jack. A People Divided: Judaism in Contemporary America. New York: Basic Books (A Division of Harper Collins), 1993; pp. xiv-xv.

[11] Occhiogrosso, Peter. The Joy of Sects: A Spirited Guide to the World's Religious Traditions. New York: Doubleday, 1996 Chapter: Judaism; p.250.

[12] Andryszewski, Tricia. Communities of the Faithful: American Religious Movements Outside the Mainstream. Bookfield, Connecticut: Millbrook Press, 1997; p. 95.

[13] Slater, Elinor and Robert, Great Jewish Men. Jonathan David Publishers, (1996) p. 279.

For my Christian readers:

The Written Law is another name for the Torah, the first five books of the Bible. The Oral Law is the Jewish legal commentary on the Torah explaining how its commandments are to be carried out.

It is possible that the early New Testament Jewish believers in Jesus are referencing these Noahide principles while attempting to give guidance to the first gentile Christians:

Acts 15:19-20:

> *It is my judgment, therefore, that we should not make it difficult for the Gentiles who are turning to God. Instead we should write to them, telling them to abstain from food polluted by idols, from sexual immorality, from the meat of strangled animals and from blood.*

It is remarkable to see our nation's recognition of the Noahide Laws, along with one of the most influential and prolific figures in 20th century Judaism, Rabbi Menachem Mendel Schneerson (1902-1994). Affectionately called "The Rebbe," Schneerson expanded the Chabad Lubavitch from a small Jewish sect to a large, powerful religious movement.

In March 1991, the U.S. Congress passed a Joint House Resolution (H.J 104) recognizing the significance of the Noahide Laws and commending the Lubavitch Rebbe for his educational outreach.

Who Is A Jew?

Traditional Judaism holds that a Jew is anyone born to a Jewish mother or converted to Judaism in a *halakhic* manner (that is, according to Jewish law). Although the Torah does not specifically acknowledge matrilineal descent as being the bloodline recognized by the Almighty for determining true Jewishness, there are a number of verses referenced by Jewish sages suggesting children with gentile fathers and Jewish mothers are considered Jews. One of them is found in the Book of Leviticus.

Leviticus 24:10-20 :

Now the son of an Israelite woman, whose father was an Egyptian, went out among the sons of Israel...

On the other hand, when dealing with Jewish fathers in Ezra 10:2-3, the Jews returning to Israel vowed to "put away" their non-Jewish wives and the children born to those wives. If these children were Jewish (the sages teach)...they would not have been "put away."

Ezra 10:2-3:

Shecaniah the son of Jehiel, one of the sons of Elam, said to Ezra, "We have been unfaithful to our God and have married foreign women from the peoples of the land; yet now there is hope for Israel in spite of this. So now let us make a covenant with our God to put away all the wives and their children, according to the counsel of my lord and of those who tremble at the commandment of our God; and let it be done according to the law."

The other point of view in this discussion is articulated well by Shaye Cohen, Professor of Hebrew Literature and Philosophy in the Department of Near Eastern Languages and Civilizations of Harvard University: "Numerous Israelite heroes and kings married foreign women: for example, Judah married a Canaanite, Joseph an Egyptian, Moses a Midianite and an Ethiopian, David a Philistine, and Solomon women of every description. By her marriage with an Israelite man a foreign women joined the clan, people, and religion of her husband. It never occurred to anyone in pre-exilic times to argue that such marriages were null and void, that foreign women must 'convert' to Judaism, or that the offspring of the marriage were not Israelite if the women did not convert."

Nevertheless, sometime during the Roman occupation and the

Second Temple period, a law of matrilineal descent was adopted, and by the 2nd century CE, it was universally accepted.

Answering the question:
"What would you say if a Jew told you he wanted to convert to Christianity?"

My answer: The Christian faith is a costly and painful one for a Jew to follow. I would certainly answer questions about my faith as I was asked to do so. Though my conversion occurred through a very private search for God, I would direct a Jewish enquirer to speak with his/her rabbi, and to read the New Testament including the passages from the Tanakh referenced throughout the scriptures.

As a Christian, I trust it is God alone who can give revelation concerning the things I believe to be true concerning Jesus of Nazareth.

Question 10

"What is your deepest prayer for the Jewish people?"

Standard Christian Answer:
Definitely the "Jesus talk."

The sanctuary was filled with Jews and Christians; the rabbi looked into the white of my eyes and, without blinking asked, "What is your deepest prayer for the Jewish people?"

And I almost went into auto-pilot and gave him the Jesus talk.

"What would be so wrong with that?" Christian readers ask.

'Think about it.

His question was filled with historic horror as well as hope, warranting much more consideration than the answer he was fully expecting to hear from me – an answer confirming his suspicions that nothing had really changed in Christianity's perception of the Jews.

"Rabbi, let me tell you a story," I suggested.

The Saban Leadership Seminar

The AIPAC Saban Leadership Seminar is the premier training event for pro-Israel college students, and I received an invitation to speak at their 2006 gathering.

219

> *AIPAC's premier student political leadership training seminar is presented through its Schusterman Advocacy Institute, and held twice each year in Washington, D.C. More than three hundred of AIPAC's top student activists from over one hundred campuses participate in three days of intense grassroots political and advocacy training. During this seminar, students meet with top Washington policy makers, elected officials, and Middle East experts. For more information, contact:oncampus@aipac.org*

The wrap-up banquet I was asked to address happened to fall on my daughter Sterling's thirteenth birthday. Before answering the request from AIPAC, I sat down, told her about the speaking invitation, and reminded her that she was more important to me than anything else in the world.

"Sweetheart, I can call AIPAC and explain to them there is no way I can be there for the event, or I can go to D.C., and we'll celebrate your birthday when I get home," I offered her.

"NO, DAD!" my precious Zionist daughter scolded me.

"You need to go, and we can have my birthday later," she assured me with a big smile.

"But you really owe me," her smile appeared to grow slightly menacing.

Jewish College Student Activists

From the intense giddiness in the atmosphere of the beautiful D.C. Hilton Hotel lobby, I could tell that the hundreds of pro-Israel college students had really been energized by the Saban Seminar. I had been moved to tears of concern numerous times in my preparation to speak at the evening's wrap-up banquet and my apprehension was only magnified as the event approached. AIPAC asked me to fill an hour, which is a very long time to listen to me; and although they had knowingly invited a Christian preacher to speak, I knew I was not there to preach.

What to do?

I was seated at the banquet with a table full of students who could not have been kinder or more engaging and my troubled heart began to calm. Before I could eat my dessert, the Master of Ceremonies whisked me to the stage and my long hour began.

There are rare moments during gatherings such as this where every individual becomes a part of the whole. No longer is a speaker addressing listeners; rather the engagement becomes a conversation with an assembly of passionate participants. That evening we experienced such a metamorphosis, during which I began to comprehend that the majority of Jewish students in attendance were not the least bit religious.

"What happened at that moment in this gathering would be my prayerful answer to the question you asked," I told the rabbi.

You Are A Jew!

"Pastor Victor," the Jewish college student addressed me as he stood.

"It is very, very hard to be a Jew on any college campus and to try and stand for Israel," he bemoaned a painful truth.

Following his statement with a question every student wanted answered, he asked, "Do you have any suggestions on what we can do?"

My response was immediate, unprepared, and seemed to fly out of my mouth like a frightened dove from a thicket.

"YOU ARE A JEW!!" I exclaimed with tears filling my eyes. "You are the firstborn of HaShem! Yours is the adoption as sons, the Divine Glory, the covenants, the receiving of the Law, the Temple worship and the promises! (Romans 9:3-5)

"Be strong, be encouraged, do not be terrified, do not be discouraged: for 'HaShem your God is with you wherever you go!' (Joshua 1:9)

"You are a Jew, and if you can't make it to synagogue yet, your rabbis will understand – but you have got to read your Bible. Until you do, you don't fully know who you are, nor do you know the power of your God!

"You must read the account of creation and your heritage in God's promise to Abraham recorded in the Book of Genesis, your birth as a slave-child nation, and your redemption in the Book of Exodus.

"You might want to skip Leviticus for a while – and nobody really likes math, so leave the Book of Numbers until you connect with a rabbi, but you must also study the Prophets and the Writings!

"Read your Bible, seek the God of Abraham, Isaac, and Jacob, and be Jews. That is what you need to do on your college campuses."

Answering the question:
"What is your deepest prayer for the Jewish people?"

My rabbi friend was crying as I finished my story. He went on to tell me how he had left his faith as a young man, and only after his father's death had he returned to the God of his youth.

"My father would have given you every last penny he had to find me and speak those words you spoke to the students," he stated with deep remorse.

"When I say such things to young Jews," he explained, "they just think, 'Oy, he's a rabbi – of course he's going to scold us!'"

"But when you, a Christian pastor, say to them..." he couldn't finish the words.

I then answered, "My friend, within that story is my answer to your question. My deepest prayer for you, and the Jewish people, is that you be good Jews. I pray that you continue to seek the God of Abraham, Isaac, and Jacob within the words of Torah, the Prophets, and the Writings.

"As a Christian, I believe every good thing God desires to reveal to either of our communities He will do so through His Holy Word. I also believe those who seek Him, find Him."

The Jews have precious promises, made to them by Almighty God.

Upon His Name He has vowed to keep them.

I believe He will.

Epilogue
One Final Story

The 2008 Christians United For Israel DC Summit had just ended.

For those of us called to labor within this movement, we had thoughts before the conference that perhaps Christians United For Israel was over as well.

Months of the most baffling and vicious campaign of lies and distortions concerning the religious beliefs of Pastor Hagee reached a boiling point with Senator John McCain chucking him and CUFI out of the window of his campaign bus.

But what the enemy meant for evil, God used for good.

Though under enormous pressure not to participate in the conference, independent Democratic Senator Joe Lieberman of Connecticut defied critics, stating his bond with Pastor Hagee is even stronger now than it was before recent controversies.

Lieberman received a standing ovation when he quoted Genesis 45:3 to the more than 4,000 attendees at the Washington Convention Center in the nation's capital, exclaiming, "I am your brother, Joseph."

He then went on to quote from the New Testament, saying, "I greet you with the greeting Jerusalem gave to Jesus: 'Blessed are you who come in the Name of the Lord!'"

A number of us at our table were soon suffering dehydration from our near non-stop, joyful crying!

Dan Gillerman, the outgoing Israeli ambassador to the United Nations, told CUFI that their love for Israel sustained him during his six years in the post.

Sitting at the table with my wife and me were two brothers who are rabbis: Rabbi Yossi is from New York and Rabbi Moshe is from Italy. Their father is the Chief Chabad Rabbi of Italy, overseeing more than 800 rabbis. They happened to have read David Brog's book, *Standing With Israel,* and could not believe what was happening in the United States concerning Christian support for the nation and people of Israel. Rabbi Moshe, from Italy, flew all night to Washington, D.C. just to see if the phenomenon was true.

The Fingerprints of God

I had been asked to be Senator Lieberman's host at the conference, so I spent the first half of the evening in the green room with him and his staff. At one point I mentioned my new friend, Rabbi Moshe, and his fact-finding journey from Italy.

Senator Lieberman's speechwriter asked incredulously, "Rabbi Moshe Garelik?"

"Yes, do you know of him?" I inquired.

"He was my rabbi when I lived in Europe and is one of the best men I have ever known!! He is here tonight?" The young staff member couldn't believe what he had just heard.

We ran out of the green room to my table where Rabbi Moshe was seated, and I looked away as they greeted each other in a supernatural and emotional reunion.

The fingerprints of God.

The banquet ended at 9:45 PM and Rabbi Moshe immediately jumped on a plane and flew back home to Italy. In an e-mail sent the next morning, his brother, Rabbi Yossi, summed up their personal experience at our summit.

Here is a small portion of it:

> *Thank you for giving me the opportunity to witness first hand one of the greatest miracles in our times. While sitting in that room, I could literally hear the footsteps of Mashiach. There is no question in my mind that this is only the beginning and in the future millions will follow. You're very fortunate to be a part of such a phenomenal event in history...."*

One of the signs of the coming of Mashiach from the Orthodox view has to do with the way gentiles will treat Jews. This is one reason why being in the midst of such pro-Israel, Jew-honoring gentiles caused my rabbi friends to experience such hope and wonder.

One biblical reference used for this belief is in Isaiah:

Isaiah 49:22-23:

This is what the Sovereign Lord says; "See, I will beckon to the Gentiles, I will lift up my banner to the peoples; they will bring your sons in their arms and carry your daughters on their shoulders.

"Kings will be your foster fathers, and their queens your nursing mothers. They will bow down before you with their faces to the ground; they will lick the dust. Then you will know that I am the Lord; those who hope in me will not be disappointed."

What the Enemy Meant for Evil...

Pastor Hagee introduced several prominent Roman Catholics who attended the event at his invitation, including Bill Donohue of the influential Catholic League. Donohue had been the most vocal critic of statements (incorrectly) attributed to Hagee that were characterized as anti-Catholic.

Weeks before our summit, Pastor Hagee asked to meet face to face with Donohue and the Catholic leadership. Their gathering ended with prayer, thanksgiving, and Pastor Hagee receiving their wholehearted endorsement after they allowed him to open the Bible and present what he actually teaches and believes.

The result is that CUFI is broadening its tent to include Roman Catholics who are now interested in joining with us in our support of Israel.

"What the enemy meant for evil, God has turned into good," Pastor Hagee reported.

Amen to that!

The next morning, our thousands of CUFI delegates had several hundred appointments on Capitol Hill, where we spoke to our representatives about passing stringent sanctions on Iran and support the nation of Israel as it fights for its existence. One of the last of the California meetings ended with Senator Barbara Boxer asking to have her picture taken with our California Christians United For Israel delegation.

Join Us Now!

If you have not done so already, join us by going to: **www.cufi.org** and adding your name and email to our CUFI Rapid Response Team. We will send you current Middle East updates and instruction on how to address the leaders of our nation on legislation affecting the nation of Israel.

Baruch HaShem!

For my Christian readers:

"Praise the Lord!"

May God bless you with everything that is good.